My Favorite Wisdom

notes to my grandchildren about life and living

R. Wayne Morgan

My Favorite Wisdom

R. Wayne Morgan

2012 Paperback Edition

Copyright © 2012 by R. Wayne Morgan

ISBN: 978–0–9845048–4–8

R. Wayne Morgan Publisher
Contact: MyFavoriteWisdom.com

All photos by R Wayne Morgan
Cover photo: Sunrise at Stanley Lake Idaho

Dedication

To Carolyn   my wife and best friend
for showing me it is never too late for love

To my parents   Dad – for teaching me to think for myself
Mom – for teaching me unconditional love

To my teachers for inspiring me to learn
Ms. Juneau, Mr. Bracone, Mr. Pribnow,
Mr. Neville, Dr. Kennedy, Dr. Choiniere
Rev. Mary, Dr. Jim

To my children for the joys of parenthood
Kirk, Ryan, Kasey, Kori

In Loving Memory of Melody

WARNING:

Reading these essays may be hazardous to your beliefs.

Belief systems are necessary for good mental health. They should be treated with respect and changed cautiously.

There have been many times when my beliefs were under siege due to new information or experiences. During such unsettling periods, my emotions ranged from heart racing anxiety to immobilizing depression. Fortunately, I have always managed to find a satisfying synthesis, incorporating my new knowledge into a worldview that made sense to me. Those moments of insight are exhilarating.

If you are satisfied with your current belief system and your beliefs are not harming others, you may not need to read further. If you are living a happy, healthy, and fulfilling life; if you are enhancing the well-being of those you love; and if your life is making a positive contribution to the planet; you may have all the wisdom you need.

On the other hand, if you are like me, you may have a deep-seated need to increase your understanding, even at the risk of feeling temporarily unsettled. I have never felt completely satisfied with my level of knowledge and I continue to be a seeker. Just be warned that increased wisdom may put old beliefs at risk.

Human knowledge and wisdom are always changing as we learn more and increase our understanding. The ideas presented here are only a snapshot of a river that continues to flow and expand.

WARNING II:

I am not a professional writer and this book has not been professionally edited. *Read at your own risk!*

Contents

Contents

Prologue

Dear Adam,

As I begin this writing,
it is nearing the end
of the opening decade
of the twenty-first century.

You have just celebrated your first birthday by covering your face with chocolate cake frosting. Actually, your mother did most of the damage because she thought it looked cute and wanted pictures. Your father was a coconspirator.

I am certain you have no memory of this event, but you may have seen the photos and wondered how you could have been so uncoordinated, even as a one year old. You were not. Blame your parents.

I am your grandfather, the one you call "Grampy." I figure that part of my job as a grandparent is to be a source of wisdom. I expected to have a lot more of it by now, but since the future is uncertain, I thought I had better pass along what I have so far.

If I am still around, I would enjoy discussing these ideas with you. If I am not able to talk with you, perhaps my written words will be helpful. Ultimately, the wisdom that works for you will come through your own explorations and experiences. My hope is that these writings may give you a starting point and a sense of direction.

With Love,
Grampy

Preface: Why do I need wisdom?

Dear Adam,

In the world today, unlimited information is available at our fingertips. Absorbing and organizing this information leads to knowledge. Wisdom, however, is a higher level of understanding. It connects knowledge to the timeless truths of our humanity.

If you are reading this as a young person, wisdom is not likely a priority for you. I can only say that if I had gotten wiser a little faster, it would have saved me a lot of struggle and pain. The value of wisdom is its ability to increase our satisfaction in life and decrease our suffering.

Wisdom leads to increased happiness and life enrichment. With wisdom, we recognize the difference between short-term desires and long-term fulfillment. Wisdom guides us to go beyond comfort and pleasure. It expands our awareness of possibility, encouraging us to make choices that lead to the realization of our potential.

Every life has painful setbacks. The greatest pain in my life was the death of my wife (your Grandmother) Melody. Wisdom gave me the courage to follow my grief to its darkest depths instead of denying or avoiding it. My previous experiences of loss had taught me that even the most intense emotional pain is temporary, and my personal growth in wisdom allowed me to look past the darkness to find the light of acceptance.

With wisdom, we internalize the Buddhist proverb, "Pain is inevitable, suffering is optional." Wisdom provides the perspective that allows us to grieve our losses, accept our disappointments, and move forward. Those without the tools that wisdom provides can become stuck in the loop of pain we call suffering.

It was twelve years between the time your Grandmother was diagnosed with an inoperable brain tumor and her death. Those were difficult years, filled with chemotherapy, surgery, radiation, hair loss, fatigue, fear, and debilitation. Your Grandmother faced it all with courage and resilience.

Challenges often speed the growth of wisdom. During those years, we developed a deep appreciation for the blessings that each day brought to us. Our time together became precious because we knew it was limited. We found the wisdom to live in a state of acceptance and gratitude.

I am sorry you have not had the opportunity to know the loving presence of your Grandmother Melody. She had a wisdom of the heart that touched all who knew her.

Wisdom grows through experience, but we can speed the process by learning from those who have come before. Some extraordinary people have gifts of vision, insight, and understanding. We can stand on their shoulders.

The following pages contain some of my favorite wisdom. Enjoy.

With Love,
Grampy

"A man is wise with the wisdom of his time only, and ignorant with its ignorance."

HENRY DAVID THOREAU

Introduction: Why does the world need wisdom?

When I was in first grade, a new student joined our class at the beginning of second semester. His name was Brian Shimamoto, and he looked different from the rest of us. Other students began to tease him at recess because of his Asian facial features. This was only a few years after the end of World War II and many adults still harbored hatred for the Japanese. Their children repeated the racial slurs they learned at home.

I remember the sense of injustice I felt as I heard the insults and watched other boys chase Brian around the playground, pushing and hitting him. I found myself joining with Brian to defend against the verbal and physical attacks. We became fast friends. When the other students finally got to know Brian, he became one of the most popular kids in school.

This might have been the beginning of my search for wisdom. I wanted to understand why people could be so mean. My mom said I was a serious child, unusually concerned with fairness and doing the right thing. Perhaps this is why my search for wisdom began at such a young age.

Growing up in the America of the 1950's, it was easy to assume that the Bible was the book that would contain the wisdom I was seeking. I set about the task of reading it while I was still in elementary school, but found it very difficult. The focus on the history of the Jewish people thousands of years ago did not seem relevant to me, and I was not mature enough to understand the deeper insights that the Old Testament has to offer.

I do not want to discourage you from reading the Bible. No book has had a greater impact on Western civilization. For its cultural significance alone, it is worth exploring. To get the most out of it, however, I recommend the guidance of a class or companion text to help you with historical perspective and allegorical interpretation. The Bible is easily misunderstood.

While I struggled mightily with the Old Testament, I enjoyed reading the New Testament. I read the four Gospels many times and felt a strong connection to the love and compassion exemplified by Jesus.

Although I was confused about certain issues—like the existence of the devil, the relationship between Jesus and God, and why Jesus had to suffer so—I did manage to distill some rules for living from the New Testament that have served me well. The words of Jesus continue to inspire me.

Even as I accepted the teachings of Jesus as a guideline for living, my search for deeper spiritual understanding continued. Like many in my generation who were not completely satisfied with the Bible as the ultimate truth, the mystique of Eastern philosophies caught my attention. I learned to meditate, practiced Yoga, attended spiritual retreats, and read the words of the great teachers of the East. My search for spiritual wisdom is ongoing.

When human populations lived in relative isolation, it was natural for them to develop their own wisdom. Such differences in belief systems have contributed to human conflicts over the centuries, from early tribal disputes to wars between nations.

The toll of human conflict has been staggering. The total dead during World War II was over 50 million, including 20 million Soviets and 10 million Chinese. These numbers dwarf the figure of 400,000 American casualties. Another 10 million, including 6 million Jews, died in Nazi death camps.

These kinds of numbers are not new to history. Tens of millions died during the colonization of Africa and Asia by Europeans and more tens of millions died during the religious Crusades of the Middle Ages. It seems that much of history is the story of war, cruelty and death.

Today, human population growth and competition for limited resources heighten tensions between countries. Intolerance and extremism in the name of religion also increase the chances of armed conflict. At the same time, the development and proliferation of weapons of mass destruction make such conflict unthinkable. Any rational evaluation leads to the conclusion that, while honoring historical and cultural differences between populations, we must adopt belief systems that promote mutual understanding.

Worldwide environmental degradation is another major issue as we begin this new millennium. Demands for rising standards of living and disregard for sustainable practices are depleting our natural resources. In order to protect our planet, it is imperative to move toward belief systems that promote respect for the natural world.

Encouraging understanding between people and caring for the environment are two guiding principles of *My Favorite Wisdom*.

I taught science for over three decades. I believe in science as a way of approaching the truth about our universe, our Earth, and the human animal. I also believe that fully understanding our humanity requires a spiritual perspective in addition to a scientific one. As Einstein said, "Science without religion is lame. Religion without science is blind." At this point in history, science and religion are often viewed as competitors for people's allegiance. For me, the search for wisdom has largely been about the integration of these two ways of understanding. This is another central theme of this writing.

Despite the formidable challenges we face, I believe there is reason for optimism. There is growing consensus, fueled by concerns over climate change, that we must move toward sustainable practices to protect our environment. As I write this, nations are just beginning to address differences in perspectives and priorities that inhibit progress toward responsible stewardship of our Earth. In addition, human population growth is slowing in many parts of the world as a natural consequence of education and economic development. In the short term, we continue to do terrible damage to our biosphere, but in the long term, these two trends may provide hope for our global ecosystem.

Education and economic development are also the keys to reducing conflict between people. The educated are less likely to hold extreme, intolerant beliefs, while economic security reduces the need for aggression.

Modern technology provides the means for transportation and communication that will bring us together as a global community. Increased understanding and acceptance between people will surely follow. Resorting to violence to resolve differences will be less likely when we are no longer strangers.

It is with considerable humility that I pass along my limited understanding. Scientific knowledge is expanding exponentially as I write these words. It is my hope that spiritual understanding will also expand, with the recognition of our common humanity helping to erode religious and cultural barriers. Like sandstone cliffs above the boiling sea, all human constructs eventually concede to the forces of nature.

May you always remain open to new wisdom. Trust your intuition, your innate inner guidance, to help you separate the flowers from the weeds. Worthy ideas will promote the highest virtues of humanity—integrity, respect, cooperation, compassion, selflessness, and love.

I. Foundations of Wisdom

Dear Adam,

When I was a child in the middle of the twentieth century, UFO's (unidentified flying objects) were a hot topic in the news. Movies depicted space aliens as monsters who wanted to capture and harm humans. I remember feeling scared when I looked up at the night sky on a camping trip—or even in my own back yard. I had difficulty appreciating the inspiring beauty of the stars because I was afraid of the unknown.

The antidote to fear is knowledge.

I have called this first section of writings Foundations of Wisdom. *It deals with the questions of how we came to be and what makes humanity unique in the world of life. I use the word* foundations *because I believe any true wisdom must be based on a clear understanding of who we are. Any reliable wisdom about the body, the mind, or even the soul must begin with a scientific understanding of our origins and history.*

Wisdom may go beyond science, but true wisdom will not ultimately conflict with science.

By its nature, scientific understanding is always advancing. New knowledge will be available to you by the time you read this, but the main concepts I discuss are so fundamental and well supported that they are unlikely to change over time.

Depending on how old you are and your background in science, these writings may be challenging or just a simple review. In any case, I hope they will serve as a good foundation for future wisdom.

With Love,
Grampy

"In the beginning God created the heavens and the Earth."

GENESIS

Beginnings: Where did the Earth come from?

I look forward to going camping with you where stars fill the clear-aired darkness and hiking with you where wildflowers and butterflies greet us at every turn. Spending some peaceful time in connection with nature can stimulate reflection on things that get overlooked in the hurried pace of everyday living. When looking at the vastness of the night sky or the beauty of a mountain meadow, it is natural to ask the big questions:

How did the universe begin? How did life begin?

The short answers are: *We don't know* and *We don't know.*

In the absence of scientific knowledge, myth backed up by the authority of tradition has always provided our only answers to these two big questions. Origin myths are universal, from the spiritual traditions of native peoples to the holy texts of the great world religions. For those of us of Judeo-Christian background, the Bible offers a familiar and poetic version in Genesis.

What does science have to say? More than you might expect. Before I begin, however, let me say something about the nature of science.

Science is a way of understanding that relies on careful observations and reasonable, logical conclusions based on those observations. Experiments (controlled observations) are repeated and conclusions challenged until scientists with the proper expertise reach consensus. Even then, the answers provided by science are always considered tentative—open to revision as required by new observations.

The key word here is consensus. Scientists often disagree as they explore new areas of knowledge and some scientists may cling to ideas that have been discredited by the larger scientific community. Nevertheless, as observations are refined and conclusions critiqued through peer review, the truth usually settles out.

Obviously, no scientists were around to observe the beginning of the universe. For a long time, it seemed reasonable to assume that our universe had always existed as it is today. Even Einstein, one of the greatest scientific minds in human history, believed this until late in his career despite mounting evidence to the contrary. Eventually, he would call this belief "the biggest blunder of my life."

Several scientists, working in the 1920's with new telescopes and measuring techniques, found strong evidence that the universe was not static, but was actually expanding. Einstein should have expected this, because gravity would logically cause a stationary universe to collapse upon itself. Today, the observation that the universe is expanding has been verified beyond debate.

By measuring the distances between galaxies and the speed of expansion, scientists have been able to calculate when the expansion must have begun. The strong consensus is that our universe came into being approximately 13.7 billion years ago.

The universe contains about 100 billion galaxies, *each* containing from *ten million* to *one trillion* stars. If you left earth traveling in any direction at the speed of light, (186,000 miles per *second*) you could travel for billions of years without reaching any edge. For all practical purposes, the universe is infinite in size.

Scientists have made tremendous advances in astronomy and cosmology in recent decades, yet even to the brightest minds on the planet, our universe still holds many mysteries.

The question of origin has led scientists to a nearly incomprehensible hypothesis. If you reverse the expansion of the universe and take it to its logical beginning, all the matter in the universe must have been originally contained in a single point. My mind is boggled as I try to think about this. It does not even seem possible. All I can say is that many physicists with a lot more knowledge and brainpower than me have come to this conclusion.

This point that contained our entire universe is sometimes referred to as the *singularity*. The singularity is a theoretical construct, but scientists generally agree that from this point, the entire universe burst forth in what is called the *Big Bang*.

In 1965, scientists aimed sensitive antennas into space and found microwave signals that actually stem from the Big Bang itself. Using evidence gathered since then, they have been able to describe the events that took place as the universe formed back to within 10^{-43} seconds (one tenth of a millionth of a millionth of a millionth of a millionth of a millionth of a millionth of a millionth of a second!) of its expansive beginning.

Of course, this does not answer the question, *What came before the singularity?* or *What caused the Big Bang?* As unsatisfying as it might be, at this point we have to be honest and say, *We don't know*.

What happened after the instant of creation of our universe is clearer. First, energy was created in the form of gravity, electromagnetism, and the strong and weak nuclear forces. Then followed ungraspable quantities of the most fundamental particles of matter (quarks, leptons), which combined to form the building blocks of atoms (protons, neutrons and electrons). Within a relatively short 300,000 years, the universe cooled sufficiently to allow the building blocks to come together to form atoms of hydrogen and helium. Within the first billion years, under the force of gravity, these atoms began to coalesce into the stars of the galaxies.

Stars shine because of the release of energy when atoms of hydrogen fuse to form atoms of helium (thermonuclear fusion). Heavier elements (composed of larger atoms) are also created in the nuclear furnaces of stars. When some stars die, they shed into space their outer layers that include some of these heavier elements. In addition, when a large star dies the core of the star collapses and the surface of the star explodes, producing a *supernova*. Again, the blown off outer layers contain many different elements.

Our sun is a medium size star. At 4.6 billion years old, it is almost half way through its radiant lifespan. In another 5 billion years, it will enter a red giant phase and begin expanding before ultimately going dark and releasing its elements. (Stars go though several stages as they use up their hydrogen fuel.)

The sun is a second or third generation star, meaning it was formed from the leftover debris of other stars. The planets of our solar system, including Earth, formed from the same debris.

Six elements—oxygen, carbon, hydrogen, nitrogen, calcium, and phosphorus—make up over ninety-eight percent of the mass of the human body. Another fifty-six elements are found in trace amounts. The atoms of all these elements were born in stars.

We are, in fact, made of stardust.

"Great indeed is the sublimity of the Creative, to which all beings owe their beginning and which permeates all heaven."

LAU TZU

Origins: How did life get started?

We have a clear idea how the universe developed after it started, although our vision is increasingly blurred as we reach back toward the actual moment of conception. What do we know about the origins of life on Earth? It turns out to be frustratingly similar. Here are some things we know.

Less than 5 billion years ago, a great swirl of gas and dust on an arm of the Milky Way Galaxy began to coalesce. Ninety-nine point nine percent of this matter became our sun, with the remainder forming larger and larger clumps that became our solar system— the asteroids and comets, five dwarf planets (including the recently demoted Pluto), and eight planets. Some scientists think that about 4.5 billion years ago, while the Earth was still hot and molten, an object the size of Mars may have crashed into the Earth, blasting out enough material to form the moon. Unable to escape the Earth's gravity, the moon began to orbit our planet. The impact may have blown the atmosphere off the Earth, allowing more rapid cooling.

In any case, over the next half billion years, the Earth cooled until it formed a surface crust. A primitive atmosphere reformed, and water (perhaps mostly from the impact of meteorites and icy comets) condensed to form the oceans.

Scientists agree that within two hundred thousand years or so after the Earth became hospitable, life had arisen. The earliest known evidence of primitive cells called prokaryotes (think simple bacteria) is dated to 3.8 billion years ago. So where did these cells come from? *We don't know.*

There are many competing hypotheses to explain how life on Earth began. Most of them are variations on a theme. Non-living chemicals (methane, ammonia, water, etc.) were synthesized into organic compounds (amino acids, nucleic acids) by intense sources of energy (lightening, UV radiation, thermal vent heat, etc). These organic compounds found their way to just the right environment (like the catalytic surface of clay or iron pyrite) where they formed polymers (long chains). Bubbles (membranes) separated some of these chains from their surrounding environment and the chains developed the ability to self-replicate. Metabolism started within the membranes and life had begun.

Yes, I know, it sounds farfetched. It is about as mind bending as the notion of the entire universe contained in a single point! Scientists have been able to synthesize some organic molecules from inorganic molecules in the laboratory by simulating the conditions of the early Earth, but they have never produced anything close to an actual living system.

In order to produce something that we might label as life, two primary ingredients are necessary. First, you need a molecule that can encode information and is self-replicating (like DNA). Second, you need catalysts (like enzymes) to speed the chemical processes necessary for that replication. DNA cannot act as a catalyst and enzymes are not self-replicating.

RNA, a molecule similar to DNA, can act as an enzyme *and* self-replicate. Many scientists now think that RNA may be the most logical candidate for the first molecule that led to life on our planet.

Recently, some scientists have seriously considered the possibility that life came to earth from outer space. Meteors and comets contain organic molecules that could have started life on Earth, or perhaps life developed first on Mars and then was blasted to earth by an asteroid impact. Of course, this just pushes back the question, "Where did *that* life come from?"

Science can only work with observable evidence. Up to this point, for the universe as well as life on Earth, the evidence of beginnings is just not available.

Great wisdom, huh? Two of the biggest questions possible and science has no answers. But don't let that sour your opinion of science. Scientists have answered many fundamental questions. I will share some of their discoveries as we go. However, I must admit that I do not expect the issue of beginnings to be settled in my lifetime, or perhaps even in yours.

I have enjoyed watching you develop your curiosity about life. As a toddler, you loved to find spider webs and search for the spider. Recently, you have been fascinated by ducks (which you can never quite catch) and colorful caterpillars (and their chrysalises above your front door). Perhaps you will become a biologist! Whether you become a scientist or not, I hope you never lose your sense of wonder about life.

The more we learn about living things, the more astounding they become. In the next essays, I discuss some of the processes that have produced the amazing variety of life on Earth, including the most unique example of that variety—humans.

In my foregoing discussions, two of the books I used for background information were *The Language of God* by Dr. Francis Collins (head of the Human Genome Project that first determined the sequence of human DNA) and *Finding God in the Questions* by Dr. Timothy Johnson (a physician who was the medical editor for ABC News). These men of science use the unfathomable nature of some of our questions about the universe and life on Earth as evidence for the existence of God. Both books are well written and worth reading, but I think this particular kind of argument raises some concerns.

People have always used God or the Supernatural as an explanation for the unexplainable. Before we understood infectious diseases, people thought that these conditions were the work of evil spirits or a disapproving God. Does this mean that we have less reason to believe in God because we have discovered pathogens like bacteria and viruses?

Any understanding of God must be built on something stronger than our need to fill in the blanks of our knowledge. Our scientific understanding is maturing and growing with each passing decade. Our spiritual understanding has to mature and grow to stay relevant. I will come back to this idea in the second half of these writings.

I want to mention here that I intentionally have kept the essays brief and I encourage you to supplement these introductions when a topic sparks your interest. I have included a bibliography as a reading resource (although by the time you read this, perhaps you can download information directly to your brain!).

In addition to the aforementioned books by Dr Collins and Dr. Johnson, I used an excellent book on the history of scientific progress titled *A Short History of Nearly Everything* by Bill Bryson. If you like science and want a deeper insight into how science makes progress, I highly recommend Bryson's book.

Evolution: Why are there so many forms of life?

Although we do not know exactly how life started, we know a great deal about how life has changed over time once it got going. Many people with traditional religious beliefs have difficulty accepting that life on Earth has evolved, even though it is one of the most fundamental and well-supported ideas in all of science.

There are several reasons for this:

1) **People have been taught to reject evolution in their churches.** It is difficult to fit evolution into your belief system if you take the Bible literally. If the only choice is between "The Word of God" and the word of scientists, scientists lose every time. Ultimately, science will win this battle, just as it did when the church taught that the Earth was the center of the universe. Religions ultimately lose credibility when they deny scientific progress.

2) **People have *not* been taught to understand evolution.** Most people in the world have limited scientific literacy. Surveys in the United States consistently show that over forty percent of the population does not believe in evolution. This makes about as much sense as saying "I don't believe that substances are made of atoms" or "I don't believe that some diseases are caused by germs." This will change as more people become better educated in science, allowing them to understand evolution and the evidence on which it is based.

3) **People think evolution makes humans less special.**
Some people feel devalued by the idea that we are related to all living things and, in fact, have evolved from other species of living things. Our language and consciousness make us unique in the world of life, but not separate from it. Rather than being a negative, I think an understanding of the role that evolution has played in our development as a species can provide us with valuable insights into ourselves.

4) **People think evolution makes God less special.**
If there are natural explanations for the heavens, for the diversity of life, and even for the development of humans, does that take away from the power of God? More simply, if everything has a natural explanation, where does God come in? The vast majority of people believe in God as described by their religion and they are comfortable with their beliefs. It will take time for the widespread acceptance of a concept of God that is compatible with our understanding of the natural world.

The lack of acceptance of evolution is a testament to the power of misinformed belief. The evidence is overwhelming that species are not fixed, but instead have changed dramatically during the history of life on Earth. Humans have even taken advantage of this ability of organisms to change. In a span of only a few thousand years (as opposed to the millions of years available to natural evolution), humans have domesticated the wild wolf (*Canis lupus*) into over two hundred breeds of dog (*Canis familiaris*). Perhaps even more dramatic has been our use of selective breeding to change one species of wild cabbage into such strikingly different vegetables as broccoli, cauliflower, kohlrabi, kale, Brussels sprouts, spring greens, collard greens, romanescu, and all of the modern versions of cabbage.

Because evolution is such a key concept, I'm going to start with a few definitions. A **population** is all of the organisms of a species occupying a particular area at the same time. The **gene pool** is the sum of all of the genes contained in that population. **Evolution** is the change in the gene pool of a population over generations.

To use a classic example, if you consider a population of giraffes in a certain region of Africa, then all of the collective genes contained in the giraffes of that population would be the gene pool. As the genes in this gene pool change over time, the characteristics of the population change. This is evolution.

Evolution is a fact. The fossil record clearly shows us innumerable examples of how species have changed and eventually spawned new species. We can even observe evolution in action in rapidly reproducing species. Darwin did not discover the fact of evolution. What Darwin did was to hypothesize the mechanism that causes most of evolution, **natural selection**.

Let us go back to our population of giraffes. The length of a giraffe's neck is the result of the interaction of many genes that the giraffe inherits from its parents (modified by environmental factors like nutrition). Within a population are distributed genes that help the neck grow longer, as well as genes that produce shorter necks.

Environmental factors can make longer or shorter necks have an adaptive advantage. For example, longer neck giraffes may have a competitive edge in gathering food from tall trees. This may allow tall giraffes a better chance at reproducing and passing on their genes for the trait of tall necks. The genes carried by shorter necked giraffes may become less common in the gene pool over many generations. Thus, we say that the population is evolving because of natural selection—nature selects the best-adapted individuals to pass on their genes. In this scenario, the average neck length for giraffes will increase.

Will giraffe necks just keep getting longer and longer? No, because having such a long neck can also have disadvantages. Perhaps a longer neck is more vulnerable to injury or makes the giraffe an easier prey for predators. There are always balancing forces at work in evolution. When longer necked giraffes can reproduce more often and contribute more genes to the gene pool, then that trait will become more common. If shorter necked individuals reproduce more, then the species will move in that direction. Changes in the environment determine which traits confer reproductive advantage.

It can be difficult to go back and reconstruct what selective pressures produced the evolution of a trait. Even though food gathering seems a logical reason for long necks in giraffes, an alternative hypothesis involves **sexual selection**. Male giraffes battle for access to females by *clubbing*, beating each other with their heads. Males with longer necks dominate such competitions and thus may pass on their genes more often.

There are other causes of evolution besides natural selection and sexual selection. **Mutations** (changes in genes) will add new genes to the gene pool. This is extremely important as a source of new traits. **Gene flow** occurs when members of a population enter or leave, also changing the gene pool. In addition, the random chance nature of reproduction (which individuals mate, which sperm fertilizes which egg) can change the gene pool. This effect, called **genetic drift**, can be especially significant if a population is small. Sometimes a rare gene may not pass to any offspring and be lost to a species forever.

Nevertheless, by far the most important contributors to evolution are natural selection and sexual selection—what scientists often refer to as *differential reproductive success*.

A common misunderstanding is that evolution is purposeful—that evolution has as a goal the production of more and more complex organisms with human beings as the crowning achievement. On the contrary, evolution involves a great deal of randomness, as an examination of life's diversity will attest. Human beings are the result of the confluence of some very unlikely events. There is no scientific evidence that our evolution was certain, and our long-term survival has never been guaranteed.

Complexity is produced by the addition of more genetic options. This occurs through the recombination of existing genes (sexual reproduction), and through the addition of new genes (mutation). When complexity gives a reproductive advantage, it is passed on to future generations. On the other hand, if a less complex trait gets the job done—maintains reproductive success—then it will *not* be replaced by a more complex option.

The vast majority of organisms on Earth are quite simple, with bacteria being the perfect example. There are an estimated five nonillion (5×10^{30}) bacteria in the world—successful in more environments than any other kind of living thing. There are ten times as many bacteria cells in your body as there are human cells.

Bacteria are perfectly content with their diverse lifestyles ranging from photosynthesis and chemosynthesis to decaying matter and (rarely) causing disease. These simple organisms do not sit around dreaming of the day they can move up to the big time by increasing their complexity. As long as they remain well adapted to their particular environment and way of making a living, evolution will not change them.

If the environment changes, however, then bacteria adapt. For example, if we develop a new antibiotic, the bacteria with the greatest natural resistance survive and reproduce, increasing the frequency of their genes in the population. Bacteria reproduce rapidly (some every twenty to thirty minutes), allowing them quickly to evolve resistance to our newest antibiotics.

If we base our judgment on the success of species, it might appear that the goal of evolution is the production of insects! From annoying ants to beautiful butterflies, over one million species of insects have been described, with estimates of total species ranging from six to ten million. Compare this to the roughly five thousand species of mammals alive today and you can see how extraordinary the success of insects has been.

"The mind cannot possibly grasp the full meaning of the term of a hundred million years; it cannot add up and perceive the full effects of many slight variations, accumulated during an almost infinite number of generations."

Charles Darwin wrote these words in the middle of the nineteenth century. Here, at the beginning of the twenty-first century, it is no less difficult to comprehend how evolution created the enormous variety of life on Earth—unless we comprehend time. Small changes in species can add up to substantial changes when they accumulate over millions or even billions of years.

Think of how many generations of organisms would be produced in a million years, a relatively short length of time in geologic history. Even if the average generational time is long— say about twenty years for humans—it means *fifty thousand generations* in a million years. If new generations are produced annually, as they are in many species, that is a *million* opportunities for subtle gene pool changes to add up, guided by natural selection.

This is why there is such a rich diversity of life on our beautiful planet. Time has allowed natural selection and other processes to produce organisms that are adapted to every conceivable environment where life can succeed.

> "... the resemblance of the enzymes of grasses to those of whales is in fact a family resemblance."
> LEWIS THOMAS

Instructions: How do genes produce traits?

I have never liked horror movies. They leave images that stick in my mind and give me nightmares. This must be a minority opinion though, because they have always been popular. Dozens of films have dealt with vampires and werewolves, based on folklore that dates back centuries. Mythology about supernatural beings that consume blood or flesh is found in cultures around the world, but stories specifically about vampires and werewolves flourished in 18th century Europe to the point of near hysteria.

No one knows how these superstitions began, but one intriguing hypothesis involves a genetic disorder called Porphyria. Individuals with this condition have an error in the metabolic pathway that produces hemoglobin, the oxygen-carrying component of red blood cells. This error causes chemicals called porphyrins to build up in the body, producing a variety of serious health issues. Some of the symptoms of this disease include:

- Extreme light sensitivity (exposure to sunlight is painful)
- Red urine and teeth with a reddish tint
- Increased hair growth on unusual places like the forehead
- Seizures and serious mental disturbances

If someone in a medieval village had these symptoms, it is easy to understand how imaginations might start to run wild.

Today we know that people with Porphyria are not vampires or werewolves (which do not exist). We understand the genetic basis of Porphyria and thousands of other disorders. We also understand how genes work when things go well, as they usually do.

I have already used the term *gene* in the last essay, assuming you know that genes are the chemical instructions that guide the development of an organism's traits. I consciously used the term *guide* here instead of *determine*, because the idea that genes act alone in producing our physical characteristics is a common misconception. It is much more complicated than that.

For one thing, the environment of an organism influences gene expression. To use a simple example, say that you have inherited genes that would normally give you the potential for above average intelligence, but you are born into an impoverished environment where you do not get adequate mental stimulation or education. Your environment may not allow your genes to express fully, resulting in lower than expected mental abilities.

One dramatic and tragic example of modified gene expression occurred during the Dutch famine of WWII. In 1944, German occupying forces restricted food supplies to the Netherlands for many months. Dutch women who were pregnant during this time were severely malnourished, and thus so were their babies. This environmental stress produced *permanent changes in the gene expression* of these children, causing them to grow up with increased risk of obesity, diabetes, cardiovascular disease, and even premature mental deterioration with aging.

In addition to nutrition, chemicals within and around each cell also regulate gene expression. Hormones are one such class of chemicals, able to influence gene expression far from the glands that produce them.

For example, the male hormone testosterone can influence the expression of the gene for baldness. If a male receives a gene for baldness from either parent, he is likely to become bald. Testosterone helps stimulate the gene's expression. By contrast, a female must inherit a gene for baldness from both parents for her to become bald. This is why baldness is more common in males.

Most of our physical traits are influenced by many genes. In the case of baldness, regulator genes turn the baldness gene on at a particular age, causing you to bald earlier or later in life. Other genes regulate *penetrance*, that is, how fully the gene is expressed (partially bald or completely bald). There are also genes that control the pattern of the baldness.

I was always comforted by the fact that my father had a full head of hair until his death at age 79. I assumed I would also avoid baldness, especially since my hair looked similar to his—dark, thick and curly. I even followed the same pattern of turning gray at a young age, just as he had (an obvious sign of wisdom).

As I matured, I was surprised when I began to see patches of red scalp showing through on photos of myself. I was even more surprised when my barber asked if I wanted to keep my hair a little longer to cover the bald spot on the back of my head! Unfortunately, my hair is following more of my mother's pattern. Her hair got very thin as she aged, to the point where she wore a wig when she went out of the house. If she had been a male, she probably would have gone totally bald.

My experience with baldness illustrates the complex interaction of genes and traits. This is an area where an introductory biology class can be misleading. (When my students applied Mendel's classic heredity rules to their own traits, I sometimes had to reassure them that they were not adopted!) Not only do many genes interact to produce traits, but factors such as nutrition, exercise, and stress can influence the expression of genes. In unexpected findings, even subtle factors like social interaction and thought processes can affect gene activity.

In one classic study, Romanian orphans with limited adult interaction were found to have stunted growth, behavior problems and increased mortality. An increase in positive attention and physical contact actually changed the balance of hormones in the children's blood, returning them to health.

As I write these words, *epigenetics* (the science of gene regulation) is one of the most dynamic and promising areas of scientific research. It is the next level of understanding we need to comprehend the complex relationship between genes and traits, including the relationship between genes and disease.

Unfortunately, some companies are using our incomplete knowledge of genes to mislead. They claim the ability to predict your chances of developing certain traits or diseases based on a genetic profile. As you can tell from our brief discussion, this is a venture fraught with potentially dangerous misinformation. At this point, I think it is wise to focus on genes as sources of potential, rather than determiners of fate.

You have probably learned in school about DNA, the chemical code that forms our genes. Here is a quick review:

DNA (deoxyribonucleic acid) is a long, thin chain of chemical building blocks called nucleotides. The chain of nucleotides takes the form of a twisted ladder (double helix), which I am sure you have seen illustrated. There are four different types of nucleotides in DNA (abbreviated A, T, G, & C), which allows them to form a code—like an alphabet with only four letters. Much of our DNA is "junk" left over from evolution; other portions are regulatory regions that guide gene expression. Less than two percent of the DNA in each of our cells forms the coded messages we call genes. Every cell in our body contains the same genes, about 20,000+ from mom and 20,000+ from dad.

As you know, cells are microscopic, yet the DNA contained in each human cell is over 2 meters long. In order to fit, the DNA coils up in the nucleus of cells, forming structures called chromosomes. Since the human body has nearly 100 trillion cells, all of the DNA in your body would stretch out to be 200 trillion meters long—a distance equal to 650 trips to the sun and back!

A human egg cell has 23 chromosomes, as does a human sperm cell. When they get together during reproduction, the fertilized egg has 46 (23 matching pairs of chromosomes). As the new human life grows, each chromosome is copied into each new cell so that every cell in the body has all 46 chromosomes contained in the original fertilized egg. In other words, every cell in the body has the same genes.

Because all of the cells carry the same instructions, the difference between a pancreas cell that makes insulin and a nose cell that helps make mucus is determined by which of the genes in each cell is active. It is as if each cell receives the same cookbook of instructions, but only follows the recipes on selected pages. Cells know where they are in the body and what their job is (which recipes to make) based on chemical messages they receive from the cells around them during development.

How does DNA tell each cell what to do? DNA controls the cell by controlling the production of proteins. You see, at one level you can think of life as an enormously complex set of chemical reactions. Enzymes (protein catalysts) control the chemical reactions of life, and genes (DNA segments) determine which enzymes are produced in any given cell.

Genes → Enzymes → Cell Function

In a pancreas cell, a group of genes guides the production of enzymes necessary to produce insulin. In a nose cell, those genes are never used, but a different subset of genes is activated which produce the enzymes necessary to manufacture components of mucus.

Of course, some chemical reactions are the same in all cells of the body, and even in the cells of different species. About 25% of genes are common to all life.

Organisms have different numbers of genes and chromosomes, but this is not directly related to size or complexity. A mosquito has 3 pairs of chromosomes while a silkworm has 28. A frog has 13 pairs, a mouse 20, a duck 40, but a cow only has 30. Corn has 10 pairs, sugarcane 40, and some ferns have over 500! The differences reflect packaging rather than function, with most organisms falling in the range of 5 to 25 chromosome pairs.

It is interesting to note that chimpanzees have 24 pairs of chromosomes compared to the 23 pairs for humans. Careful analysis has shown that somewhere in evolutionary history, two of the chromosomes found in chimps fused together in our ancient ancestor to form one chromosome. The species that first carried this new chromosome (labeled chromosome #2 in modern humans) is long since extinct. Yet this new configuration has been passed along to us, carrying genetic messages to us through millions of years of evolution.

While each species has different numbers of genes and chromosomes, the DNA code is the same for all forms of life—from bacteria to whales, from algae to redwoods. This is the most powerful evidence for the relatedness of all living things.

"We must not say every mistake is a foolish one."

CICERO

Variation: Why do we all look different?

As natural selection has written the book of life, mutation and recombination have provided the creative muse.

Through the eons, the Earth has been characterized by change. Continents have drifted, mountain ranges have lifted and eroded away, ice has moved over the land—only to be replaced by hot desert sands. Although the changes may seem slow from our human perspective, changes in geology and weather have always been a challenge to life on our planet. *Variation is life's insurance policy for success in an ever-changing world.* Individuals of any species show variation in their traits, increasing the chance for survival and reproduction of some members as the environment inexorably changes.

Life has two main strategies to insure variation within species, sexual reproduction and mutation.

Sexual reproduction guarantees shuffling of the genetic deck with each new generation. The importance of sex is evident when one considers the extraordinary lengths species go to in order to bring together the genes of different parents.

Strategies for sexual success vary, from the production of enormous quantities of sperm and egg when fertilization is external, to complicated reproductive structures and behaviors that guide sperm to egg inside the protective body of a female.

Plants, rooted to the ground, have had to employ wind, birds, insects, and other sexual helpers—all to make sure that sperm (contained in pollen) meets egg. Animals accomplish the same results with remarkable sexual displays and mating rituals.

Some species can reproduce asexually, but these species often have the ability to use sexual reproduction when the environment allows. Even single cell bacteria, which just divide to reproduce, have a strategy to pass DNA from one to another. This allows them to exchange genes and develop new combinations of traits without sperm and egg.

Plants have a life cycle that alternates sexual and asexual phases. Most of the green plants we see around us are the asexual stage, while the sexual stage is limited to small growths within the confines of a flower or cone. The pollen grains that cause allergic reactions in so many people are actually the tiny sperm producing stage of the plants life cycle.

If you choose to have more than one child, it will become clear how effective the genetic shuffle can be in producing variation in traits!

The other strategy for producing variation is mutation. Mutations are changes in DNA, commonly the result of copying errors or environmental factors like chemicals and radiation. Mutations alter the coded genetic message, and thus alter the enzymes that run the cell.

If this happens to the DNA of a body cell, then only that cell and its descendants will produce the faulty enzyme. The result of this kind of mutation is most often innocuous, perhaps killing the one cell or causing a localized change (like a patch of gray hair or skin discoloration). At the other extreme, mutations can be deadly for an organism, as when they alter the regulation of the cell division cycle and turn a normal body cell into a cancer cell.

From the standpoint of evolution, the mutations in sperm or egg cells are of the most concern, because they are added to the gene pool and may be passed down through generations.

Since organisms are so complex and tightly regulated, mutations that are inherited (thus part of every cell in the body) are usually harmful and sometimes fatal to the individual. These mutations are removed from the gene pool because they detract from an organism's chances for reproduction. Occasionally, however, mutations can provide positive options for species adaptation.

If a mutation produces a trait that helps an organism adapt to its environment (enhancing its chances for reproductive success), the new gene increases in frequency in the gene pool. These new traits accumulate over tremendous spans of geologic time until a species has undergone dramatic changes or even given rise to new species.

The chemical errors that become mutations are surprisingly common, but the cell has proofreading enzymes that usually correct mistakes as soon as they occur. Only about one out of every 100,000 mistakes makes it past this check system. However, if mutations are usually so harmful, one might reasonably ask why natural selection has not perfected the process to one in a million or one in a billion. The answer may be simple. Some reasonable error rate is actually desirable—because variation is desirable. You might say *nature makes mistakes on purpose.*

Support for this idea is found in mechanisms that cells have for actually *creating* mutations and new combinations of genes. One form of recombination involves the *crossing over* of chromosomes during the cell division that produces eggs and sperm. In this process, chromosomes break, rearrange themselves, and then rejoin to form chromosomes with new combinations of genes— and sometimes mutations.

In addition, there are genes, called *mutators*, which manipulate the copying errors of other genes and *transposons*, which remove themselves from one location on the chromosome and then insert themselves into another—again, sometimes causing mutations.

The next time you see someone who looks unusual or behaves strangely, just keep in mind that nature loves experimentation!

To show the power of relatively small changes in genes, consider an enzyme called *lysozyme* found in saliva, tears and mucus. It helps prevent infections by breaking down the cell walls of bacteria. In the ancestors of modern day ruminants (grass eaters like cows, horses, sheep, etc.), a mutation produced an extra copy of the lysozyme gene. This gene, altered by further mutations, produces a lysozyme that can survive the acid environment of the stomach.

Most animals cannot digest the cell walls (cellulose) of plant tissue—what we call fiber. Ruminants, however, with this altered form of lysozyme, can live on the relatively low nutritional value provided by grasses. They grow bacteria on the grass in their digestive tract and then feed on the bacteria. Their final stomach chamber produces this new form of lysozyme (which remains functional in an acid environment) that digests the bacteria, releasing the nutrients to be absorbed by the animal.

Not only did this mutation produce a variety of grazing animals that have been important to human nutrition, but also the grasses themselves are an evolutionary adaptation to the selective pressure of the ruminants. Some plants (through mutation and natural selection) developed the ability to grow from the bottom up instead of at branch tips like most plants. This allowed them to survive grazing. They became our modern day grasses, many of which produce highly nutritional grains.

It may be fair to say that without the error that produced ruminants, grasses like wheat, oats, barley, rice, and corn would not have evolved—and agriculture, the foundation of civilization, would not have developed.

Sometimes a simple mistake can have profound consequences.

"Distant relatives are the best kind—and the further the better."

KIN HUBBARD

Relatives: How am I similar to other primates?

I love going to the zoo. (I hope we have had the chance to go together a few times.) I especially enjoy the monkeys and apes. There is something fascinating about watching our closest relatives in the animal world, the primates.*

What makes something a primate? The hallmarks are a highly developed brain with complex social behavior, excellent binocular vision, and grasping hands. The principal groups are lemurs, monkeys, apes, and humans. All of the special traits of primates developed as adaptations to an arboreal (tree-dwelling) existence, even though some species (like us) no longer inhabit the trees.

What would start a species of mammal on the path to "primatehood?" As always, it is the impact of the environment on variation. The ancestors of primates were small insect eaters that lived in the tropical and subtropical forests. For over fifty million years, natural selection worked with the raw materials of mutation and recombination to mold the primates to succeed in their forest habitats.

As the gene pools of primates changed in response to the selective pressures of life in the trees, certain traits emerged. Eyes became forward facing and snouts reduced to allow binocular vision—a life-saving asset in judging the distance to the next tree limb.

---

* Of course, I would rather see animals in their natural habitat, but many high quality zoos are doing a service for wildlife through research, breeding programs, and public education.

37

Dexterous hands with opposable thumbs were valuable for grasping branches, food, and fur (think of a young primate clinging to a parent). Nails on sensitive fingers with independent control replaced claws. This permitted the plucking of insects, the pealing of fruit—and the social grooming of companions.

Primates rely heavily on learning and most often give birth to single young that have a prolonged period of maternal dependency. Parental care is essential for young animals in the trees and primates are among the most attentive parents in the animal kingdom.

In addition to the bonds of parental care, primates show extensive *sociality* (a tendency to form and associate in social groups) based on kinship networks. Relatives recognize and act preferentially toward one another, a phenomenon that makes perfect evolutionary sense. Relatives share a percentage of their genes, so helping a relative to survive and reproduce increases the frequency of one's own genes in the population.

Note that this is not a conscious act on the part of an individual primate. Genes influence social behavior, and natural selection can act on behavioral traits just as it does physical traits. For example, beavers placed in a bare, unfurnished room will engage in all of the normal behaviors associated with dam building. They place ghost sticks into a ghost dam, just as if they were working with real wood in their natural water and forest environment.

Behavioral tendencies are hard-wired into the brain. Natural selection will act on these tendencies just as it does on physical traits. Thus, the gene variation that causes a primate to help its relatives will become more common in the gene pool—because the relatives probably carry the same gene! In addition, your relatives will help you in return (reciprocity). Social behavior (along with manipulative hands) may have spurred an increase in brain size in primates to twice that of a typical mammal.

Perhaps because of their reduced weaponry and relatively small size, primates often work together for defense and food gathering, developing intense social bonds—even between non-relatives.

The social interaction between members of any primate group usually strikes a balance between **cooperation** *and* **competition**. Successful competition can confer a reproductive advantage to individuals and thus their genes become more common in the gene pool. But cooperation can also be an adaptive trait. For example, male-male bonds underlie many complex primate behaviors, including cooperative hunting and defensive patrols. Such cooperation allows all members of the group to increase their chances of surviving and reproducing.

This tug of war between cooperative and competitive behavior is played out in human lives as well. Parents are universally vexed as they watch their children playing cooperatively and sweetly one minute, then chasing and hitting each other the next. Corporate executives may cooperate to complete business projects, then "stab each other in the back" as they compete to climb the ladder of success. (The duel motivations of cooperation and competition are a central theme in understanding human behavior. We will revisit this in future essays.)

Of all the primates, we share the most genetically and behaviorally with the apes, particularly chimpanzees. One area of higher cognition observed in chimps is called *theory of mind*—the ability to take into account another individual's mental state. Chimpanzees, for example, warn companions who lack knowledge of impending danger, but do not bother warning those who are already aware of the danger. They take into consideration what is in the mind of another and adjust their behavior accordingly. Chimpanzee mothers are even able to recognize the areas of ignorance in their offspring. They can thus focus their attention and energy on teaching to those areas.

In addition to developing theory of mind, chimps display a high level of empathy for their companions. They will lick the wounds of another who might be injured, but ignore similar wounds of individuals who are no longer alive. In one classic case of observed empathy, chimps chased away members of the group who approached the dead body of a companion, but allowed a sibling of the dead individual through to mourn the loss.

Of course, humans have taken the ability to develop theory of mind and empathy to entirely new levels.

A word of caution is necessary here. It is incorrect to assume that traits and behaviors seen in monkeys and apes represent early steps on the way to human traits and behaviors. Keep in mind that we did not evolve *from* modern primates, but only share common ancestors with them back millions of years ago. Evolution has taken each primate species on their own journey to the forms we see today in response to available variations and localized environmental pressures.

We do share, however, the *roots* of certain traits (like sociality) that are ancient in primates. These may provide some insights into the evolution of our own species. Perhaps this is why the primate exhibits at the zoo hold such fascination for most visitors.

Apes use gestures that are intentional and iconic (i.e. they depict the actions that companions should take). They even string gestures together in meaningful sequences. Only humans, however, can generate and comprehend the complex syntax required for spoken language, because this form of communication required the evolution of anatomical and brain changes that no other primate has. Because it enhances sociality, communication is one primate trait that blossomed in humans.

Along with efficient bipedal locomotion, the ability to use language clearly separates us from our primate relatives. Language is not only the basis of efficient communication in humans—it is the foundation of complex thinking.

"Humans are not proud of their ancestors, and rarely invite them round to dinner."

DOUGLAS ADAMS

Ancestors: Why are we different from apes?

Primate evolution provides an example of the power of mutation and its impact on the history of life. Increased body size can be an adaptive advantage in survival and reproduction. But it can also create problems for tree dwelling animals—smaller branches will not support you and balance becomes more difficult. In Central and South America (by random chance), mutations occurred which led to the development of a prehensile (grasping) tail. By aiding in locomotion in the trees, this extra appendage allowed an increase in size in New World monkeys.

Meanwhile, in Africa and Asia, the mutations that produce a prehensile tail never occurred or at least never took hold. Instead, Old World primates had mutations that helped them develop longer arms and modified shoulder joints. These changes allowed larger bodied primates to develop in this region because they could swing below the branches (brachiating) instead of climbing on top. As they became larger, some began spending more time on the ground. These adaptations eventually lead to a new line of primates, the apes, our closest evolutionary ancestors.

The great apes include orangutans, gorillas, chimpanzees, and humans. All share the traits of longer arms, lack of tails and larger body size than most monkeys. The evolutionary line that became the apes separated from other primates about 15 million years ago. The gorillas started on their own evolutionary path five million years later. Because of their powerful bodies (which eliminate most concern about predators) and abundant food sources, gorillas have less need to be nimble of mind than chimpanzees.

41

By contrast, chimpanzees, which branched off about seven million years ago, rely on their intelligence and social skills for defense and food gathering. Their brainpower is evident in their social interactions, problem solving ability and use of tools.

Much has been made of the genetic similarities between chimps and humans. Recent completion of genetic sequencing of both species shows 35 million base (nucleotide) differences between our DNA and that of our closest living relative. While this represents many mutations over the millennia, it still means that about 98.8% of our 3 billion base pairs remain the same. Of these differences, scientists think that only a few thousand are biologically significant. We are ten times more closely related to chimps than rats are to mice.

Differences in genetic sequences, however, do not tell the whole story. Minor changes in regulatory regions of our DNA produce major changes in physical features and mental capacities. A single regulatory gene mutation may have doubled our brain size. Even though humans have a common ancestor with modern apes, millions of years of separate evolution have made us unique.

The fossil record has been slow to reveal the details of human evolution because of two basic problems. First, the populations of our ancestors were always small as they struggled for survival in a dangerous and competitive world. Total populations ranged from the tens to hundreds of thousands, not likely reaching a million worldwide until after the development of agriculture some 10,000 years ago. Second, it takes an extraordinary sequence of unlikely events to produce a good fossil—and extraordinary luck to find it. It is estimated that the odds of one of our ancestors leaving behind fossil evidence of itself is less than one in a million.

As we start this new millennium, we do have enough fossil evidence to provide an outline of our ancestor's story, although exact dates and lineage continue to be debated as more evidence is accumulated. Here are some highlights:

As mentioned, our last common ancestor with chimpanzees lived about seven million years ago in Africa. During the next four to five million years after the split, our ancestors (collectively referred to as hominids) increased in stature, developed enlarged brain size, improved their bipedal locomotion, and lost body hair (a possible adaptation to a warming environment).

Several hypotheses have been proposed to explain the development of the human trait of upright walking. Many scientists believe it was an adaptation to a drying African climate that created open savannahs—grasslands with reduced tree density. Others consider the freeing of the hands for exploring and carrying things to be key, or perhaps lifting up on hind limbs for better visual scanning to spot predators. Some suggest that upright stance was adaptive for reaching seeds and berries, squat feeding, or sexual display. Most likely, some combination of these factors played a role in this evolutionary turning point.

Other primates can manage to walk on two legs for short distances, but only humans have developed the changes in body structure necessary for efficient bipedal locomotion. The importance of this trait cannot be overstated. As biologist Stephan Jay Gould famously put it, "Mankind stood up first and got smart later."

The limb on the tree of life leading to humans had many side branches—species that succeeded for hundreds of thousands of years before becoming extinct. One species that lived for a million years and represents a milestone in evolution is called *Homo habilis* ("handy man"). This probable ancestor shows up in the fossil record about 2.5 million years ago and is similar enough to modern humans to be placed in our same genus. *Homo habilis* is the first hominid to show the use of simple stone tools. Its brain size was about twice that of earlier hominids, although still only half that of modern humans.

Homo erectus ("upright man") appears in the fossil record just under 2 million years ago and survived for over 1.5 million years. Its brain size overlaps the modern human range, although the average is smaller. Advances of this group include much more sophisticated bi-faced tools such as the hand axe. Although adapted for dissipating the African heat with a tall, thin stature and long, slender limbs, *Homo erectus* learned to live in caves or huts, clothed themselves in animal skins, and developed the control of fire. Intelligence and social cooperation allowed them to be the first hominids to migrate out of Africa.

Homo erectus was successful in spreading throughout Africa, Asia, Europe and Australia. One reason for their expansion and success may have been an increased reliance on meat, a food source with high caloric and nutritional value.

You may have heard of one descendant of *Homo erectus* called *Homo Neanderthalensis*, which appeared in Europe about 130,000 years ago. Neanderthal remains were first unearthed in 1856. A French anatomist reconstructed a model from the skeleton that depicted a shambling, brutish and unintelligent creature—our stereotype of a "cave-man." Unfortunately, the skeleton was affected by arthritis and the anatomist allowed his preconceived notions of what a primitive man should look and act like to influence his interpretation.

Although the Neanderthal skull is primitive looking with its low forehead, large brow ridges and enlarged nasal area, they had bigger brains on average than modern humans. Adapted for the cold with short, stocky and extremely strong bodies, they walked with a modern gait and were excellent hunters. Evidence suggests they were highly intelligent with advanced cultural behaviors, including ceremonial burial of the dead. Neanderthal DNA, recently retrieved from fossils and sequenced, indicates they may have had light skin and red hair.

Meanwhile, back in Africa, a new *Homo* species was evolving.

"The family is one of nature's masterpieces."

GEORGE SANTAYANA

Family: How am I related to all other people?

At nearly the same time that Neanderthals were developing in Europe (less than 200,000 years ago), modern humans developed in Africa, probably from a branch of *Homo erectus* stock. Between 60,000 and 40,000 years ago, following a major ice age, members of this new species called *Homo sapiens* migrated around the world. They reached Asia 50,000 years ago, Europe and Australia 40,000 years ago, with some reaching as far as Japan and Siberia by 30,000 years ago. During another ice age about 16,000 years ago, sea levels dropped three hundred feet and modern humans were able to cross a land bridge between Siberia and Alaska, spreading south throughout the Americas.

Although scientists are still debating the extent of any interbreeding that might have occurred, there is general agreement that modern humans replaced the Neanderthals and other descendants of *Homo erectus* by out competing them. Thus, *Homo sapiens* became the last hominid left on earth.

Our success as a species was by no means assured. Some 70,000 years ago, a six-year volcanic winter followed by a thousand-year ice age nearly drove *Homo sapiens* to extinction. In what biologists call a "population bottleneck", the number of humans on the planet may have dwindled to less than 20,000 individuals.

So if we are one species, descended from common ancestors, why do people around the world look so different? As always, the answer is variation and natural selection. First, let me emphasize that the most striking characteristic of human beings is our similarity rather than our differences. In fact, most anthropologists do not consider "race" to be a biologically valid term, but rather a distinction created by culture.

Because we descended from a small group of ancestors, we are one of the most genetically homogeneous species on earth—99.9% genetically identical. There is 2-3 times more variation among chimpanzees and 8-10 times more variation among orangutans.

In addition, of that small amount of variation between humans, 85% exists within any local population, 7% between populations on the same continent and only 8% represent differences found between continents. In other words, there is likely to be just as much genetic difference between two Scandinavians as between an African and a Scandinavian. So why are we instantly aware of differences between "racial groups?" Obviously, the so-called "racial" differences we note are in easily observed traits like skin color and facial features.

Many genes influence human skin color, including four to six that specifically control the production of melanin. Melanin, a pigment that darkens the skin, comes in two forms, red and dark brown. The degree of expression of all of these genes combined with environmental factors (like sun exposure and diet) determines the gradient of human of skin color that we find around the world.

Modern apes have light skin under their hair, and it is assumed that early hominids did as well. As our ancestors evolved bodies with less hair (perhaps for more efficient cooling by perspiration), darker skin became adaptive as protection from the strong ultraviolet light of tropical Africa.

Some studies have shown that ultraviolet light reduces levels of folate (a B complex vitamin) in light-skinned people. Low levels of folate in pregnant women are associated with often-fatal neural tube defects in newborns. This could have been an important natural selection pressure in tropical climates with intense sunlight, increasing the genes for dark, protective skin color in the human gene pool.

Humans that migrated to higher latitudes were subject to different selection pressures than were present in Africa. For example, light skin allows for more production of vitamin D in climates with reduced sunlight. Two different mutations for lighter skin occurred in humans, one in East Asia and one in Europe. Natural selection increased the frequency of these new genes in those populations.

One supportive piece of evidence for this hypothesis is the fact that women, on average, have lighter skin than men do. This may be required to enable synthesis of the higher levels of vitamin D necessary during pregnancy and lactation.

Despite such logical sounding evidence, not all scientists have reached consensus on the evolution of skin color. Because human populations were generally small, some of the observed differences in appearance among peoples may be the result of random genetic drift. Other scientists suggest that sexual selection may have played a significant role, with certain characteristics becoming desirable in a particular culture, influencing mate selection and reproductive success.

As with skin color, adaptive hypotheses have been offered for changes in facial features. A thinner nose may have provided warming of cold air in northern Europe. An epicanthic skin fold of the upper eyelid (almond eyes) may have developed in Asia to protect from snow reflected sunlight, cold winds, or blowing sand.

Some genetic differences between groups of people are related to geographic or cultural isolation. For example, mutations that cause certain genetic diseases have become more common in ethnic groups that have tended to mate together for generations.

The most common serious genetic disease in the United States is cystic fibrosis that causes potentially lethal mucus build up in the lungs, digestive tract, and other organs. One out of twenty-five people of northern European ancestry carry the recessive gene.

In Tay-Sachs disease, a faulty enzyme causes physical and mental deterioration, leading to death in the first few years of life. Jewish couples whose ancestors lived in central Europe are 100 times more likely to have a Tay-Sachs baby than are other couples.

Another common inherited disease called sickle-cell anemia affects one out of 400 Americans with recent ancestry from tropical Africa. Although the condition is life threatening when an individual inherits a defective gene from each parent, individuals with only one faulty gene have resistance to malaria. In regions where malaria was common, this produced strong selection pressure in favor of an otherwise harmful gene.

On a less serious note, most mammals (including humans) lose the ability to digest milk sugar after childhood, a condition called lactose intolerance. A mutation that allowed adult digestion of milk spread through ancient dairy farming populations of Northern Europe. Today their descendants are much less likely to suffer digestive consequences when they consume dairy products.

With global migration, "racial" distinctions will become less pronounced in future generations. Today, it remains important to keep in mind that the characteristics we share in our human family are much more significant than any superficial differences in appearance.

To emphasize our family connection, consider the astounding finding that the Y chromosome in every male alive on the planet came from a single male that lived as recently as 60,000 years ago. Studies also show that the mitochondrial DNA of all humans can be traced to a single woman who lived near the dawn of our species.

All humans alive on earth today are very closely related, descendants of a small population of *Homo sapiens* that developed in Africa. To put it another way, *all the peoples of the world truly are our "brothers and sisters."* I consider this one of the most valuable pieces of wisdom I can share.

Language: What makes us a unique life form?

Evolution gave you your body (for better or worse). It is, however, more than your physical form that separates you from other animals. Your ability to speak is a key to your uniqueness.

I am sure you can think of many animals that communicate. From ants to whales, animals coordinate their activities through chemicals, sounds, movements and displays. Yet no other animal can share complex ideas, speak of the abstract, or discuss past, present, and future. More than our bipedal locomotion or grasping hands, language is what sets *Homo sapiens* apart from all other species.

We have tried to teach other animals to speak. Chimpanzees have been raised from birth as family members with all the same verbal attention and training as human babies, but they never develop spoken language. They don't have the equipment. Human babies are born programmed for language with brain areas wired to understand and produce syntax. Our nervous systems are built to allow coordinated control of breath, tongue, mouth, and lips. Our vocal cords are constructed and positioned to make speech possible.

So why do humans have language? Early hypotheses focused on the evolutionary advantages of exchanging information about the physical environment. Sharing knowledge about how to make a tool, where to find good hunting, or the location of a dangerous predator would surely provide an adaptive advantage.

More recently, however, scientists are emphasizing the need for language among hominids for social bonding. This idea is supported by studies of both tribal and modern societies, which show that most conversations are not about helpful knowledge, but rather about social situations within the group.

Monkeys and apes use grooming (stroking, scratching, massaging) to support cohesion within large social groups. Beyond picking off parasites, grooming creates trust and builds alliances that enhance status and well-being in the group. It also reinforces male-female mate bonds. Chimpanzees engage in ecstatic bouts of grooming for hours when an old friend rejoins the community. Angry adult males also use grooming to calm emotions after an aggressive outburst. Grooming serves as a commodity, exchanged in the group for other resources like food or sex.

Grooming is very relaxing, releasing endogenous opiates in both the groomer and the groomed. These internally produced pleasure chemicals are nature's way of encouraging behaviors that increase the individual's chances for survival and reproduction. Primates sometimes fall asleep while being groomed and human blood pressure drops while petting a dog or cuddling an infant. *Because of its key role in social bonding, grooming is a fundamental component of primate societies.*

Time devoted to social grooming in monkeys and apes corresponds directly to group size. The larger the group, the more grooming is necessary by each individual in order to maintain social stability. Because of the biological demands of feeding, traveling, resting, etc., no species has been observed to spend more than 20 per cent of its waking time on social interaction, including grooming. This places an upper limit on the size of primate groups that can be maintained as a cohesive unit at between fifty and seventy individuals.

Humans were able to increase this stable group size with a new form of social grooming—*conversation*. One of the driving forces for the development of language by humans was the advantage of larger bonded groups. Larger groups (as long as they remain socially stable) have advantages for food gathering and protection and offer greater genetic variation.

One way of looking at speech then is to consider it as *grooming at a distance*. Human group size increased because language allowed the "groomer" to interact with several individuals simultaneously and to reach more individuals in a day. Studies of traditional societies place a limit of about 150 individuals in a tribe before it splits into smaller groups. Studies of modern groups—communes, Christmas card lists, acquaintance webs, and internet social networks—average around the same number. When social groups exceed about 150 individuals, behavior and social contracts cannot be managed by peer pressure alone—you need a police force.

Further evidence for the key role of grooming in primates is the almost direct relationship between neocortex (frontal brain) size and social group size from monkeys to humans. The bigger the normal group size, the bigger the brain. Apparently, keeping track of social information (gossip) increased an individual's chances for survival and reproduction. Thus, increased brain size and intelligence was selected for in our primate and hominid ancestors.

A major factor in this need for increased brain capacity is the adaptive advantage of the awareness of *intentionality* in those who form our social group. Which of our allies can be trusted to come through for us in a crisis? Who might be plotting against us behind our back? Is my mate faithful? Is someone coveting my mate? Perhaps the fascination that many people find in soap opera and "reality" entertainment is a reflection of our natural tendencies to develop a *theory of mind* (what are they thinking and feeling?) about our social companions.

Fossil evidence shows that the nerves that regulate breathing and control tongue and lip movements increased in size about half a million years ago (during the time of *Homo erectus*). Changes in the position of the larynx, necessary for vocalization, occurred in a similar period. Genetic evidence for mutations (FOXP2 gene) that allow for grammar and syntax do not appear before 200,000 years ago, nearer the time that *Homo sapiens* was first evolving. This invites the possibility that wordless vocalizations preceded modern speech for social bonding.

One candidate for this vocal bonding is music—communal singing without grammatical language. There are several threads of evidence for the ancient roots of music in humans. Music is universal in peoples the world over and is always associated with deeply emotional rituals and celebrations. The high that is often felt after communal singing (whether it be in church or at a rock concert) is the result of endorphin release—just as is experienced during the social bonding of grooming. We can sing while we work and we can sing with more than one individual at a time, thus expanding the group size that can be supported by this form of bonding.

Musical sense is based in the right hemisphere of the brain as opposed to language that resides in the left hemisphere. This supports the idea that music exploits much older, more primitive neural mechanisms. It seems reasonable to imagine that communal singing may have provided a transition on the way to more complex language—we sang before we talked. Both group singing and language provide stability in larger social groups.

Language is more than a convenient communication tool. Not only is it the way we construct and experience our individual lives, but it joins us together in families and communities. Language is at the root of our sociality and our uniqueness as human beings, bonding us in ways that no other primate can experience.

"I can go further, and assert that nature without culture can often do more to deserve praise than culture without nature."

CICERO (106 BC – 43 BC)

Culture: Why have humans been so successful?

The dictionary defines culture as "the integrated pattern of human behavior that includes thought, speech, action and artifacts and depends upon man's capacity for learning and transmitting knowledge to succeeding generations." More simply, it is the rules for social behavior and ideas about our world that we pass consciously and unconsciously to our children.

Culture is a new form of adaptation that has allowed for the tremendous success of our species. No longer are we dependent on genetic mutation and recombination to adjust to our changing environment. Instead, accumulated knowledge has allowed us to modify the environment to suit our needs.

Some scientists are using the term *meme* to talk about units of culture that get passed along in cultural evolution, much as genes get passed along in biological evolution. (I don't know if this term will stick in the science vernacular, but I will use it in this writing.) A meme can be knowledge, like how to make a steam engine or launch a satellite into orbit. A meme can also be established beliefs or rules of behavior, like the status of minorities in society or the acceptability of premarital sex.

Knowledge memes arrive in the culture through scientific discovery and invention, providing new options for human adaptation. In turn, new technologies often require the development of new behavioral memes. For example, the invention of the cell phone has produced a host of new memes dealing with its appropriate use in various social contexts: Do we answer a call when we are talking with someone else in person? Do we answer during a meeting? While we are driving?

Memes used to be more localized, perhaps even limited to one town or region of the country. I remember as a freshman student at Stanford we were advised to "dress up" if we were going to San Francisco. The meme of the time was a more formal dress code in the City. By the time I left the Bay Area five years later, the "hippie" movement had transformed the dress code in most of San Francisco to sandals and tie-died T-shirts! Yet, many areas of the country were untouched by this particular change in culture.

One characteristic of memes is their high degree of "heritability." Children tend to adopt their parents' religion, political views, and leisure interests with a high degree of reliability, higher than for many biological phenomena.

Another characteristic of some memes is their persistence. Consider the formal fashion memes for high-heeled shoes for women or neckties for men. These have survived several generations in the face of obvious discomfort and impracticality— a testament to the power of cultural memes. Other memes, like the wearing of hats, seem to come and go with the decades.

Institutions tend to be conservators of memes, protecting their own survival by resisting change. By their nature, they respond slowly to environmental shifts and they have a vested interest in maintaining the status quo. For example, hospitals maintained the use of hand written charts for patients long after digital record keeping was universally available. In my own experience, schools relied on "ditto" copies years after photocopies were the standard in the business world. We still showed films when the world had moved on to digital video.

This resistance to change often brings institutions into conflict with other forces in society. Religious institutions are noteworthy examples, clinging to ideas that have been supplanted by advances in science or insisting on behavioral guidelines that are no longer supported by the cultural memes adopted by the majority.

Institutions developed by society for positive purposes can often become *iatrogenic*, that is, they can cause unintended and even opposite consequences. For example, hospitals can spread disease, prisons can produce skilled criminals, and religious institutions that espouse goodwill can teach intolerance and hate. Government programs for temporary welfare can support memes that enable intergenerational poverty. Certainly, a poorly run school can decrease a child's ability and desire to learn.

Advancements in communication speed and scope are affecting the stability and persistence of cultural memes. Knowledge, beliefs, and social norms are changing at a dizzying pace as telecommunications and social media spread new memes at the speed of light.

One factor behind this phenomenon is a significant difference between genes and memes—horizontal transmission. Genes are only passed vertically, from parents to children. Memes can be passed through the culture from peer to peer.

In the past, memes most commonly passed from generation to generation (like genes). This tended to reinforce parental authority and respect because the older generation were the "keeper's of wisdom." They had the knowledge and experience which, when passed on, could increase the success and status of young recipients. Whether in the form of farming and craftsman skills, or business knowledge and personal connections, this wisdom reinforced the status of elders in the family and in the community.

As technological advances have accelerated the speed of communication and knowledge transfer, the value of the wisdom keepers has diminished. The essential knowledge is viewed as *new* knowledge, and young people are more likely to acquire this from peers rather than from elders. Now, it is the parents who often ask their children for knowledge—to learn how to use the latest technology.

I have to wonder if this devaluing of the elders in society might have negative consequences. Experience does provide learning opportunities. If young people fail to take advantage of the wisdom developed by previous generations (not about technology, but about life), will they be destined to repeat the same mistakes? (Aren't you glad your reading this book!)

So what determines how cultural trends change? Sociologists have noted that certain individuals within any social group take the lead in spreading cultural change. They have the social status or "cool" that makes others emulate their behaviors and adopt their beliefs. Advertisers are anxious to learn more about who these people are and why they have such influence. To this point, they have tapped media and sports celebrities to help sell their products, but every social group has such leaders and advertisers are scrambling to learn to identify and use them.

Caution: Just because something is popular or common in the culture does not mean it is beneficial for individuals or the larger society. Corporations, marketing firms, politicians, and others are developing sophisticated ways to shape the culture to their own advantage. *Look carefully at new ideas and fads to avoid being manipulated.*

This first section of these writings has been focused on the question "Who are we?" I have briefly explained that we are our biology, as shaped by evolution. Yet we are more than our biology. We can only be understood in the context of our culture.

Biotechnology is giving us the power to understand and control the genes we have inherited through biological evolution. Perhaps we are at a point when we can consider actively controlling our cultural evolution as well. The first step is to acknowledge how cultural memes shape our beliefs and behaviors. Then we can consciously use our power of choice to adopt memes that support the best qualities of the human species.

II. Body Wisdom

Dear Adam,

I am on a solo hike in a magnificent redwood canyon on the Big Sur coast of California at the age of thirty-six. Walking in nature is spiritually inspiring for me, and I am enraptured by the sights, sounds, and smells that surround me. To my right, the steep canyon wall is covered with delicate, dark green ferns. Overhead are ancient towering redwoods reaching up to a vibrant blue sky. On my left is a rushing stream with its water leaping off boulders and plunging into sand lined pools.

As I hike deeper into the canyon, it gradually forms a narrow V with polished rock walls on both sides. I am too hypnotized by the beauty around me to notice that my path is disappearing as it climbs higher and higher above the dancing water. When I finally become aware that the trail has withered to a four-inch ledge thirty feet above the cascading stream, fear brings me back to consciousness. I pause to consider the wisdom of turning back.

Then suddenly a clump of moss slides beneath my foot. I turn my body toward the rock face and reach out, but there is nothing to grab. I am instantly falling at breakneck speed with my fingers bouncing off the rock in a desperate attempt to slow my descent. It is of no use. My overwhelming feeling on the way down is one of complete helplessness.

I hit bottom in a bone jarring collision with solid rock. My legs instantly collapse so that my buttocks and spine absorb the brunt of the impact.

By some miracle, I have not broken any of my trembling bones—but I am hurting. As I sit on a rounded boulder with my feet in a shallow pool of cold water, I am dazed and immobilized. Pain and gratitude alternately grab my attention as I become more acutely aware of my body than I have ever been in my life.

We tend to take our body for granted when we are young. I hope it will not take a serious accident or illness for you to appreciate the wonderful gift that it is. Your body deserves to be treated with care and respect.

With Love,
Grampy

Vestiges: Why do I get goose bumps?

Evolution does not always clean up after itself. The traces of our evolutionary history are evident throughout our bodies. Sometimes organs or structures that no longer serve their original function may develop new functions, but other times they just become vestigial. (Mutations and recombinations are random!) Vestigial organs and behaviors are those that have lost all or most of their function through evolution. It is important to remember that evolution affects only those traits that increase or decrease the chances for reproduction.

The classic example for humans is the appendix, a vestige of a digestive organ called the cecum. Our herbivorous ancestors, like many herbivores today, used the cecum to help digest cellulose. When the diets of our distant ancestors changed, the appendix lost this function, but remained as an organ. Despite the occasional infection that we call appendicitis, the appendix was not detrimental enough to reduce the chances for reproduction, so it never disappeared. Some scientists maintain that the appendix continues to play a positive role in the immune system, or serves as a reservoir of helpful digestive bacteria.

Perhaps no vestigial structure relates us to our ancestral past as clearly as the coccyx or tailbone. All mammals have a tail at one time or another. The tail is most prominent in humans in the one-month-old embryo, and then gradually disappears. Rarely, human babies are born with a tail, but usually bones of the coccyx become hidden from view during fetal development. Our tailbone has lost its original function of assisting in balance and mobility, but because it still serves as an attachment point for some muscles, we have not lost it.

61

Other examples of human vestigial structures include wisdom teeth (which often fail to erupt properly), ear muscles (which only a small percentage of people can activate), and the *plica semilunaris* (a small fold of tissue in the corner of the eyelid that is the remnant of a protective membrane).

Goose bumps are an example of a vestigial behavioral response. Erector pili at the base of hair follicles contract to raise the hair on the body, producing the characteristic bumps on the skin. A possible function in ancestors with more hair would be to make the body appear larger under threat of predators. Additionally, it may have served to ward off cold, increasing insulation with a trapped layer of air under the hair. Both cold and fear can lead to goose bumps. Of course, the hair itself relates us to our mammalian ancestors.

Another behavioral response is the strong grip of newborn babies. Obviously useful in our primate ancestors whose young needed to cling to a parent's fur as they moved in the trees, over 35% of today's newborns can still support their own weight while clinging to a rod.

At the chemical level, most mammals have an enzyme that allows them to synthesize vitamin C (ever see a lion eat an orange?). Primates, including humans, have a gene mutation that prevents us from making the enzyme. The remains of the gene are still present in the human genome as a vestigial genetic sequence.

Evolution is always a compromise, working with existing organs and structures and available genetic changes. Some of the body modifications that took place on the way to our becoming human have created problems. Many of these relate to our unique locomotion style of bipedal walking. Problems with hips, knees and feet are common, especially with advancing age. Upright walking (not to mention sports!) takes a toll on these structures that have been modified by evolution.

Bipedal walking also required a crucial function change of the spine, shifting from a horizontal beam to a vertical weight-bearing column. The S-shaped curve that aids movement and flexibility also puts considerable strain on the five lower vertebrae (lumbar) and the seven neck vertebrae (cervical). Our spine is not perfectly adapted to our upright posture, resulting in back and neck problems. Sixty-five million Americans suffer from back pain, the second most common complaint heard by physicians.

Sinus problems are another common complaint, the result of drainage holes positioned near the top of the sinus cavities. This would work great if we still walked on all four limbs!

The primate larynx serves to open and close the air passage to the lungs, preventing choking on food. As humans developed language, the larynx moved further down the throat where it is better adapted for making the sounds of speech. Unfortunately, this decreases its effectiveness as a valve. Human babies are born with the larynx in its higher animal location to allow them to nurse without choking. Between ages three and four, the larynx drops, allowing better speech, but also making us the animal with the greatest risk of choking to death. Apparently, the advantages of language outweighed this slight increase in death rate.

The larynx undergoes a second drop and enlargement in teenage males in order to deepen the voice. It is speculated that a deeper voice increased sexual attraction to females (being a signal of larger body size or perhaps increased testosterone).

The most dramatic example of the convergence of conflicting evolutionary trends is human birth. On the one hand, the development of complex language and social skills strongly selected for increased brain size in humans. On the other, the development of upright walking required a modification and strengthening of the pelvis, which reduced the opening of the birth canal. Ouch!

Death of the mother is rare in primate childbirth, but was much more common in humans before the development of modern obstetrics. A two hundred pound gorilla mother usually gives birth to a four-pound baby. A one hundred pound human mother often gives birth to an eight-pound or larger baby—with a much bigger head—through a much smaller pelvic opening. Today, over one fourth of all births in the United States are by cesarean section.

One adaptation that has resulted from this evolutionary conflict is a modification of the newborn baby's skull. Bones are soft and pliable with gaps between the skull plates to allow the head to mold to the best shape possible to exit the birth canal. Depending on the amount and duration of pressure, skull bones even may be squeezed to overlap. Of course, the odd shaped head of many newborns returns to a more pleasing rounded shape soon after birth. The bones eventually form rigid joints between the plates to provide the solid protection of the skull.

Evolution has left our bodies imperfect.

At the other end of pregnancy, virtually all women in all cultures experience some degree of morning sickness (nausea and food aversion). This is usually confined to the first trimester, a time when the fetus undergoes critical organ formation. Some anthropologists believe that the foods most available to our ancestors contained high levels of toxins that could be dangerous to the fetus. Morning sickness may be an adaptive response to protect the delicate fetus during this vulnerable time.

Will morning sickness disappear as a human trait since our food supply is safer now? Evolution will decrease morning sickness in humans only if women who do *not* experience it add more genes to the gene pool than those who do. Check back in a few hundred thousand years!

"In our innermost soul we are children and remain so for the rest of our lives."

SIGMUND FREUD

Neoteny: Why am I curious about the meaning of neoteny?

One book I found fascinating was *Growing Young* by Ashley Montagu. In it, I discovered a concept that was altogether new to me (as it probably is to you)—*neoteny*. Although this biological concept can apply to many species, Montagu's definition is specific for humans. Neoteny "is the retention into adult life of those human traits associated with childhood." It can also refer to the extension (slowing down) of the phases of development from birth to old age. Offering support from several areas of research, Montague makes the case that we are programmed by natural selection to remain childlike in many ways.

His rationale for the hypothesis is as follows: In animals that produce several young at a time (most species), competition for nourishment both before and after birth is intense. In this case, genes favoring rapid development would be adaptive. Humans, normally having one child per birth, would be subject to the exact opposite pressures. In our case, the longer the single offspring is preserved in the womb or suckled by a protective mother, the greater the chance it will survive to maturity.

Selection pressures for delayed maturation continue after birth. Survival of *Homo sapiens* has always been dependent on intellectual curiosity and behavioral flexibility—traits of childhood. Other hominids may have gone extinct precisely because they became too rigidly adapted to local environments or specific food sources. Humans, by contrast, retained the ability to adapt to new circumstances—migrating to new habitats, discovering new food sources, or inventing new technologies as required.

Consider the traits associated with childhood: curiosity, imagination, flexibility, open-mindedness, playfulness, energy, experimentation, receptivity to new ideas, eagerness to learn. The ability of humans to retain these traits into adulthood has been essential for our species success. Plasticity and educability are the most neotenous of traits. To put it another way, the specialty of humans is non-specialization.

This extended childhood may also help explain the differences in appearance of human beings compared to other animals. Our appearance is more like a young chimp than a mature chimp. Louis Bolk, Professor of Anatomy at the University of Amsterdam called this *fetalization* and said, "Man, in his bodily development, is a primate fetus that has become sexually mature."

Some of the traits of an immature primate that are retained in adult humans include flat-facedness, minimal body hair, relatively large brain size, and pelvic structure. Bolk saw human evolution proceeding not with the acquisition of new features, but rather the preservation of infantile and juvenile traits into adulthood.

We now know that relatively minor changes in the epigenetics of development would allow humans to retain the adaptive physical and behavioral traits of the juvenile into the adult form. Although our species did not evolve *from* juvenile chimpanzees, they do provide a reasonable model of how the juvenile form of our common primate ancestor may have looked and acted.

In addition to providing the adaptive advantage of curiosity and learning, neoteny may have been encouraged by sexual selection. Mate selection is influenced by attractiveness, and many studies of human preferences indicate that juvenile facial features are considered attractive, especially in the female. Women judged to be pretty or cute typically have a rounded, flat face with small, rounded nose, set off with large eyes and full lips—all features characteristic of children. Women's efforts to accentuate these features have built the cosmetic industry.

In fact, these features are characteristic of the young of many species and generate the typical caring response we have to puppies and kittens and as well as human babies. The doll and stuffed-toy industries have taken full advantage of our innate response to these cuddly, childlike features.

Popular culture recognizes the attractiveness of juvenile features in both language and song. "Babe" and "baby" are common teams of endearment, and many popular songs have incorporated these words. Both men and women tend to use childlike talk and playfulness as expressions of loving affection because they elicit reciprocal care-giving behaviors.

It is easy to understand the adaptive advantage of our caring response to childlike features and behaviors. Parents, as well as other adults in the community, are vital to the survival of humans who remain juvenile for such an extended time. Evolution would naturally encourage such responses because caring parents and communities would produce more offspring that would survive to sexual maturity.

It is an interesting fact that humans are the only creatures who weep, that is, who shed tears during emotional distress. An infant's principle means of attracting adult attention is crying (as any parent knows). The extended dependency of human children may have led to crying as a means of eliciting parental protection and care. Another positive selection pressure might have come from the fact that human tears contain a greater concentration of the germ fighting chemical lysozyme than any other mammal.

Adult crying has taken on a broader communication role. It has become a socially cohesive behavior with expressions ranging from the sympathy of shared sorrow to the elation of shared joy. The universality of shedding tears in all human cultures indicates a profound biological basis.

With roots in the infant's appeal for help and comfort, the behavior of adult weeping emphasizes our social interdependency and our compassionate nature.

I am willing to admit that I "cry at commercials." It is not just sadness that moves me. My eyes well-up for expressions of parental love and romantic love; for heroic patriotism and noble self-sacrifice; and for stories of human triumph over adversity. My tears seem to serve as a barometer of the highest human virtues, a subconscious recognition of my connection to humanity.

There is a difference between being *childish* and *childlike*. The immature behaviors and attitudes that we label as childish do not speak to our highest nature as human beings. On the other hand, I admire a mature and responsible adult who manages to retain the childlike qualities of inquisitiveness and wonder. People are at their best when they maintain the youthful abilities to play, explore, learn, and appreciate life with enthusiasm.

Not only has the retention of childlike traits helped us to adapt and survive as a species, but also, in the words of Dr. Montagu, *the spirit of the child is, in the profoundest sense, the spirit of humanity.*

I hope that you will not confuse growing up with the abandonment of the neotenous traits that separate us from the other animals. Strive to be always *growing young*.

"God created sex. Priests created marriage."

VOLTAIRE

Mating: What makes me attracted to some people?

The biological goal of mating is straightforward: to leave as many grandchildren as possible to contribute to the gene pool. I say grandchildren to emphasize that producing offspring is not enough—they must be reproductively successful as well.

Better quality genes usually translate into offspring that are more successful. Both males and females use body symmetry as a clue to the quality of genes carried by a potential mate. Individuals with symmetrical facial features are consistently rated as more attractive by both sexes.

Symmetrical males also tend to be more aggressive and better competitors, factors that might enhance their status in the group and thus their desirability as mates. Women also report a higher frequency of orgasm with symmetrical males, a fact which would increase sperm retention and thus reproductive success.

In addition to symmetry, women generally prefer masculinized features. High prenatal levels of testosterone serve to organize male facial features in a particular way, promoting a more angular shape with exaggerated jaw and cheek structures. Unexpectedly, these males also have a longer ring finger when compared to the index finger. Women subconsciously associate these markers with genes for superior health and group status.

Indeed, men with these masculine features do claim increased social status. They are on average more aggressive, have higher musical ability and sports aptitude. They are even more successful stock traders! As you might expect, testosterone-affected males do have more reproductive success.

There is some evidence that females can judge male quality by smell as well as vision. Women who are near the most fertile part of their menstrual cycle prefer the smell of T-shirts worn by symmetrical (attractive) men, while those who are in a less fertile stage or who are using oral contraceptives show no preference.

Some studies show that females prefer the scent of partners with different MHC (major histocompatibility complex) genes than their own. These genes are related to immunity, so it would make sense for a woman to select a father for her children who would provide a more diverse mix of resistance to infections. Interestingly, women using oral contraception (and hence not fertile) do not seem to show this scent preference for complimentary immunity genes.

Because of basic biology, females and males have different reproductive strategies to maximize their contribution to future gene pools. Males consistently express a preference for women who possess traits correlated with fertility—namely youth and beauty. Youth is vital because women become less fertile with age. Beauty is a general marker for quality genes and vigorous health. I mentioned in the previous essay that men find youthful neotenous traits attractive.

In polygamous societies, aging men progressively target younger women. In societies where monogamy is the meme (social convention), men either choose younger mistresses or divorce and remarry younger wives. Data from populations around the world show that spousal age difference typically increases as husband's age at marriage increases. In tribal societies, men pay a higher bride price for younger and healthier women. Failure to bear children is the main grounds for divorce (and bride price refund) in these cultures.

While men are primarily attracted to youth and beauty (as markers of healthy reproductive potential), women are much more likely than men to prefer mates with wealth or status. In addition, they want men who are willing to invest in the relationship. Again, it is basic biology. Males will tend to maximize their gene pool contributions by increasing mating opportunities. In contrast, females maximize their contributions by selecting mates who will stay committed to the relationship and have resources to invest in child rearing.

Women in many cultures show a tendency to marry up the social scale, often compromising desires for attractiveness and youth for the security of provisioning for her offspring. One strategy for mate selection that is more common in females is "coyness". If a male shows patience in waiting for the female to consent to copulation, he may be a better bet as a faithful husband.

These differences in mating priorities between males and females are supported by much scientific evidence, from observations of the behavior of tribal peoples to analysis of postings on dating web sites. In addition, studies of sexual jealously find that males are likely to express concern about sexual fidelity, whereas females are more concerned about the emotional and resource investments that their partners make in other women.

Are humans fundamentally monogamous or polygamous? The answer may be a little of both. Most human beings live in monogamous relationship. Yet, many more cultures allow polygamy than insist on monogamy (83% of 849 societies studied). Even where monogamy is the legal norm, serial monogamy and extra marital relationships are common. Some have argued that if humans were naturally monogamous, then legal enforcement of marriage laws would be unnecessary.

From a biological perspective, animals that show sexual dimorphism (where males are larger than females) are usually polygamous. Larger male size is advantageous when there is intense competition for females. This would imply at least a mild degree of polygamy in our immediate evolutionary past. In addition, polygamous primate species have much larger testes relative to body size than monogamous primates. (Greater quantities of sperm improve the odds of impregnating more females.) Again, humans fall somewhere in the middle of the continuum, indicating a mild level of polygamy has been typical in our ancestors.

Population studies from around the world indicate that nearly ten percent of children have genetic fathers different from the father on their birth certificate. From a strictly evolutionary point of view, this makes sense. Males maximize their genetic contribution by mating with more women while females maximize their genetic contribution by seeking out the best genes they can find—even if they do not belong to the male who is providing them resources.

All this might be interesting, but how does it qualify as wisdom? The wisdom lies in the fact that knowledge is power—the power to make better choices. We are different from other animals because we are *aware of*, and thus *responsible for*, our actions.

While we acknowledge that we are attracted to appearance for biological reasons, we can choose a mate based on additional factors that may lead to a more deeply satisfying long-term relationship. While we understand our biological drive for sex, we can choose our behavior based on our values—considering the effects of our choices not only on ourselves, but also on our mate, our children, and our larger community. For humans, biology does not have to be destiny.

> **"Enjoy present pleasures in such a way as not to injure future ones."**
>
> SENECA (5 BC – 65 AD)

Pleasure: Why does sex feel so good?

Pleasure is nature's way of encouraging us to do the things that help us survive and reproduce. As you might imagine, the pleasure systems reside in some of the oldest areas of the brain, underscoring their pivotal role in our evolution. Much remains to be understood about the pleasure centers and reward circuits that motivate our behavior. Several brain structures and multiple brain chemicals work together to produce feelings of pleasure and the cravings associated with them.

One example of the relationship between pleasure and the survival of our ancestors involves food choices. Humans tend to crave and enjoy sugar, fat and salt. Think of some of our guiltiest food pleasures and they usually revolve around some combination of these three. Candy is sugar and fat, donuts are sugar and fat, potato chips and buttered popcorn are essentially salt and fat delivery systems. We know that these are not the healthiest food choices, so why do we seek them out? The answer lies in the perennial scarcities of our hominid past.

Sugar and fat are rich in calories, food energy that was often in short supply in a hunter-scavenger-gatherer society. Pleasure motivated our ancestors to seek these high calorie foods, thus enhancing their chances for survival.

Salt is essential to our body chemistry because our blood has a similar composition to seawater. (Can you see the evolutionary connection? Life evolved in the sea, and all living things carry that legacy.) Our ancestors had to seek sources of salt to maintain proper body chemistry.

Modern industrial societies provide food supplies with more than sufficient calories and salt, so our cravings now tend to work against our health instead of for it. About two thirds of Americans are overweight, with half of those being obese. Childhood obesity is also rising. While multiple factors, including our sedentary lifestyles, contribute to these statistics, our evolutionary past is partly to blame.

We can also thank corporate America. Food manufacturers and restaurateurs are well aware of our biological cravings. Fast foods, snack foods, and other highly processed foods are intentionally formulated to boost sales by feeding our desires for sugar, fat, and salt. The health implications are obvious.

Sex is the most powerful natural pleasure. This makes perfect sense considering the central role of reproduction in natural selection. I'm sure you do not want your Grampy telling you about sex. To use a phrase that is popular now, that would be "TMI!" (Too Much Information!). Besides, the way that our culture is moving, you can probably get all of the information about sex that you need from television (or intervision or webmedia or whatever you call it by now).

Our society seems more and more sexualized. Marketing companies and media have long recognized the power of sex to sell products and entertainment. In the last few decades, changes in cultural values have increased our daily exposure to sexual images. Even today's newscasters are sexy! I hesitate to imagine how sexualized the culture will be by the time you read this.

If you lived next door to the aroma of a steak house or donut shop, it might increase your food cravings. I have to wonder if living in our sexualized society similarly increases our sexual desires. Not that there is anything wrong with sex in the right context. My concern is about sex used to manipulate, since it is such a powerful component of our behavioral motivation.

There is no such thing as a safe day. When I taught health education, I used to drill this sentence into my students. I wanted them to know that (contrary to popular myth) a woman can become pregnant on any day of her menstrual cycle. Also, there is no such thing as a birth control method that is 100% effective. Couples must always be aware of these facts when choosing sexual activity.

In addition, one in four American teens contracts a sexually transmitted disease each year, and half will have one by age 25. Most STDs are viral and incurable, some deadly. Learn the facts.

At what age should one start having sex? It is not a matter of age. It is a matter of maturity. Since sex can *always* lead to the beginning of a new human life, a couple should not be having sex until they are mature enough to be responsible for a pregnancy. Since sex is intimate, you need the maturity to deal with the emotional consequences for you and your partner. Since STDs are so common and dangerous, you need to be mature enough to use proper protection—and be tested if necessary.

Sex with the right person at the right time is one of the great joys of living. Don't take the risk of ruining that potential.

We might consider excitement to be the third side of the pleasure triangle, along with food and sex. In a society that is generally predictable and safe, having an adrenaline rush seems to be an increasingly popular diversion. Participation in extreme sports, daredevil stunts, and adventure travel is increasing. Action and horror movies, video games, and virtual realities supplement life experiences. Adrenaline, endorphins, and other hormones produced by these activities stimulate our pleasure centers. They also act like narcotics, temporarily reducing pain and discomfort (an adaptation to allow successful fight/flight responses).

Enjoying food, sex, and excitement is perfectly natural. The wisdom comes in balance and moderation. Unfortunately, there are forces at work today that may upset this balance.

Moderation is not a highly valued virtue in our culture. Instead, corporations push excess—because it brings in more money. Just as reproduction is the basis for natural selection in organisms, profits drive the evolution of business. In what might be called *unnatural* selection, successful corporations grow and give birth to new corporations. Businesses that fail to make money become extinct. Decisions are based on the bottom line of the corporation and its executives, not what is best for individuals or society.

Corporations will always use pleasure and the expectations of pleasure to sell products and services. The science of neuromarketing—using an understanding of the brain to sell products—is in its infancy. Being aware of our innate reward circuits may help us enjoy a more balanced life and avoid manipulation.

Individuals are responsible for creating the society that they want, a society that brings out the best in human potential rather than pandering to its base desires. Just as we moderate natural selection with medical interventions to fight disease and death, we may also moderate the unnatural selection of corporate culture with informed choices. Four quotes summarize my point here.

"Men seek but one thing in life—their pleasure."
— W. Somerset Maugham

"Advertising may be described as the science of arresting the human intelligence long enough to get money from it."
— Stephan Leacock

"Do not bite at the bait of pleasure until you know there is no hook beneath it."   — Thomas Jefferson

"Every time you spend money, you are casting a vote for the kind of world you want."   — Anna Lappe

Seek your pleasures wisely.

> **"Every form of addiction is bad, no matter whether it be alcohol, morphine or idealism."**
>
> CARL JUNG

Drugs: How could I get addicted to chemicals?

No grandparental advice would be complete without a word concerning drugs. I have seen too many lives ruined by chemicals to remain silent. My college roommate became addicted to amphetamines and dropped out of school. Alcohol destroyed the marriages of several of my relatives and friends. My cousin died at a young age of drug related heart damage. A drunk driver killed my brother. Nearly every family in our society has suffered the devastating effects of drug abuse and addiction.

You would think that seeing the number of celebrities whose lives have been ruined by substance abuse would serve as clear warning. It seems, however, that powerful forces are at work to lead young people down the path to drugs. In this case, the desire for pleasure and our need for social acceptance and group status work against us. Curiosity and the impulse for experimentation, qualities that have helped humans to succeed as a species, operate in this context as a detriment to the individual who is uninformed.

Peer pressure is the greatest factor of all in the motivation of drug use. Peer pressure is not your friend trying to get you to try drugs. Peer pressure is a much more subtle and subconscious force. It results from the innate human desire to fit in and be accepted in ones peer group. Nothing has to be said for peer pressure to influence behavior.

Pleasure is powerful. Scientists implanted tiny electrodes into the pleasure center in the brains of rats. The rats could control the release of their own pleasure chemicals by pushing a lever. They would repeatedly press the lever in preference to food, water, and even caring for their young, until they would die of exhaustion.

Drugs affect human pleasure circuits in similar ways. Of course, their use does not always lead to death, but every drug has the potential to decrease health and well-being by altering brain chemistry. Most drugs are addicting or habit forming.

The brain consists of nerve cells called neurons, connected at gaps called synapses. When a nerve impulse reaches the end of a neuron, chemicals called neurotransmitters are released into the synapse. The neurotransmitters attach to receptors on the next neuron, triggering the continuation of the nerve impulse. Drugs produce their effects by interfering with or enhancing these chemical events in the synapses between neurons, increasing or decreasing the transmission of nerve impulses.

Dopamine is the neurotransmitter that is most involved in the reward and pleasure circuits. When released in a neural pathway, it produces feelings of pleasure and satisfaction. Lack of transmission in these pathways produces dissatisfaction and cravings. People with a genetic variation that reduces the efficiency of dopamine receptors in the synapse are more prone to risk taking, novelty seeking and impulsive behaviors as they attempt to produce more dopamine release in their pleasure circuits.

When some drugs of abuse are taken, they cause the release of *two to ten times* the amount of dopamine that natural rewards do. The brain responds by producing less dopamine, or by reducing the number of receptors that can receive the dopamine signal.

Thus, over-stimulating the system that rewards our natural behaviors produces the euphoric effects sought by drug users, but it also changes the natural reward circuit. Drugs are then required just to bring the dopamine function back to normal and even larger doses are required for the original high—an effect known as *tolerance*. This leads to dependence on the drug—what we call *addiction*.

Marijuana and opiates like codeine and heroin have chemical structures that mimic neurotransmitters. They alter normal brain function and artificially stimulate pleasure circuits.

Amphetamines, cocaine, nicotine, and caffeine are stimulants. They cause increased neuron firing by releasing abnormally large amounts of neurotransmitters, preventing their normal recycling in the synapse, or increasing receptor sensitivity on the receiving neuron.

Alcohol, barbiturates, and tranquilizers inhibit neurotransmission. The reduction in neuron activity causes the characteristic sedating effects.

Most of the above were accidentally discovered from natural sources by previous generations. With increased understanding of the brain and neurotransmitters, designer drugs will undoubtedly be manufactured to produce specific desired effects. Their synthetic origin will not necessarily change the potential for abuse and addiction.

Alcohol is a special case among drugs because of its long history and widespread social acceptance. Even though one third of Americans never drink at all, its use on social occasions is nearly universal in our culture.

The physical effects of alcohol (ethanol) are well known. They include altered perception of time and space, reduced motor skills and equilibrium, followed by sedation. Although alcohol has definite effects on the brain—it can lead to unconsciousness and even death in high doses—some of the social effects may be the result of cultural expectations.

In societies where intoxication is believed to lead to aggressive, sexual, or rowdy behavior, people tend to act that way when drinking. In other societies, where the belief is held that alcohol consumption leads to relaxation and tranquil behavior, it virtually always produces those outcomes.

A commonly held belief in our culture is that alcohol leads to disinhibition, allowing otherwise "unacceptable" behavior. Yet in societies where this belief is not widely held, such behavior is rare.

Men tend to become more aggressive when they think they are consuming alcohol, even when the drinks contain none. They become less aggressive when they have alcoholic drinks but are told they are nonalcoholic. Both men and women report feeling sexually aroused when they falsely believe that they have been consuming alcohol. Clearly, expectations influence the social effects of alcohol consumption. *You do not need alcohol to feel or behave any way that you want.*

The chances for addiction or abuse of any drug are affected by genetic differences between people (variation!). Reactions to drugs differ at the level of the synapse. It is impossible to predict whether an individual who experiments will be able to stop drug use or will be destined to become dependent.

Due to a learning process called conditioning, environmental cues become associated with the pleasures of the drug experience, triggering uncontrollable cravings. This learned response is so strong that it can reemerge even after many years of abstinence. This is why those addicted to drugs have such a difficult time staying drug free.

If abuse is defined as drug use that has a detrimental effect on important areas of life like health, family, job, etc., then nearly one in five Americans abuse drugs at some point during their lifetime. Drug abuse accounts for forty million cases of serious illness or injuries in the U.S. each year, leading to over five hundred thousand deaths and costing the economy almost half a trillion dollars.

This is one piece of wisdom you don't want to learn by experience. Please respect your body and protect your mind by avoiding the abuse of any drug.

"Be careful about reading health books. You may die of a misprint."

Health: How should I care for my body?

Loving or praying, working or playing, all the good things in life go better with health. The young take health for granted. The middle aged do not think they have time for healthy habits. The old wish they had been smarter when they were young and middle aged.

We stand on the brink of a new age in the prevention and treatment of disease. Scientists are developing a pill that simulates the benefits of exercise without breaking a sweat and another that increases the body's production of HDL (good cholesterol). Vaccines are under development for many of the world's most dreaded infectious diseases from malaria to AIDS and powerful new antiviral medications are being tested. Cancer treatments are now tailored to the molecular fingerprint of an individual's tumor. Scientists have even altered the genes of a mouse to make it resistant to all forms of cancer. Targeted gene modification will soon begin to reduce the incidence of hereditary diseases.

Health, however, is more than the absence of disease. It is a state of vitality and possibility. The key is not just to prevent illness or postpone death—it is to be capable of living life to the fullest. Even in an age of advanced medical science, healthy habits will make a positive difference.

Taken together, the practices listed below will drastically increase your chances of remaining healthy. Notice I said chances. People who never smoke get lung cancer. People who run marathons have heart attacks. Healthy habits, however, dramatically increase your *odds* of avoiding disease and remaining vital into old age—with minimal effort.

Don't use tobacco products.

I hope that by the time you read this smoking is something you only see in old movies. No single health habit has more serious health consequences. Some studies indicate that nicotine is as addictive as heroin, and for some people the process of addiction begins with the first cigarette. This is one time where your life can literally depend on your ability to resist peer pressure.

Be physically active.

Nothing adds to your vitality like exercise, and you do not have to be a marathon runner or triathlete to benefit. As little as twenty minutes of cardiovascular exercise, three times a week will produce most of the benefits for both body and brain. Mix in some strength training and stretching and your body will be ready for all the adventures that add zest to living.

Eat nutritious foods (including breakfast!).

A healthy diet, combined with no smoking and regular physical activity can eliminate 80% of cardiovascular disease and 70% of some cancers. Good nutrition may mean that sometimes you eat for health rather than always eating for pleasure. Few people eat perfectly, but staying conscious of your food choices will be well worth the effort.

One important thing to learn in order to make healthy choices is the difference between the three main types of fat. Saturated fat (from animal products) and trans fat (in processed foods) both contribute to artery clogging bad cholesterol (LDL). Limit your intake of beef, use nonfat dairy products and watch the fat content of prepared foods.

Unsaturated fats usually come from plant sources. They actually provide a cardiovascular bonus, increasing good cholesterol. Vegetable oils like olive and canola are particularly beneficial, along with the oils found in some nuts.

Fruits and vegetables are rich in vitamins, minerals, and fiber. Another excellent choice is whole grain, which also contains both nutrients and fiber. Limit refined sugars and white flour products that contain few nutrients and produce spikes in blood sugar. Limit salt intake which can elevate blood pressure. Having fruit and whole grains for breakfast is a great way to start the day, with numerous studies showing significant health benefits from regularly eating a nutritious breakfast.

Be health aware.

Other beneficial health practices include maintaining appropriate weight, developing positive social relationships, and getting enough sleep (self-discipline and the power of habit can be helpful here). In addition, ten to fifteen minutes a day of sun exposure stimulates vitamin D production, but otherwise skin should always be protected from damaging ultraviolet radiation.

Many authorities recommend taking a multivitamin as nutritional insurance. Vitamins and minerals act to help enzymes to do their job of catalyzing the chemical reactions of the cell. Extra vitamins do not make you healthier (and can be toxic), but a lack of vitamins can limit optimal health.

Finally, having appropriate lab tests and physician visits can catch health problems early and allow for effective treatment. Doctors can also provide informed advice about specific practices, such as taking a daily aspirin tablet or omega three supplements for cardiac health.

Avoid health fads that are not based on sound science.

I have notice a trend, with increasing numbers of ads and infomercials for food supplements and pills that guarantee to increase your health, energy, sexual response, and brainpower. Skepticism will keep you just as healthy—and save you money.

The claims may be supported by "clinical trials" or "scientific breakthroughs", but the positive health effects of these products are on the bank accounts of the promoters. Trust your doctor and unbiased scientific resources, not the unsupported claims found in advertising or on the internet.

Use the power of habit.

The health guidelines I have listed are probably not new information for you. The problem is in the implementation. When our pleasure circuits foil our attempts at healthy choices, the solution may lie in the power of habit.

It can be difficult to start a new habit, like getting enough sleep, eating a nutritious breakfast every day or exercising regularly. Once a routine is established, however, the power of habit can work in our favor. Choosing enjoyable foods and activities can add to motivation, as can working on health habits with a partner or group for support.

Good health habits have already saved my life at least three times. Regular visits to a dermatologist led to the discovery and removal of five skin cancers, including an often-fatal melanoma. Scheduling a colonoscopy at an appropriate life stage led to the removal of polyps, early colon cancer.

A few years ago, I experienced a 100% blockage of my main coronary artery (LAD). Although I had severe heart attack symptoms, I did not die because my healthy habit of regular exercise created collateral circulation. (Blood vessels had grown from other areas, providing the affected heart muscle with an alternate pathway for vital oxygen.) I produce naturally low levels of HDL (good cholesterol) which contributed to coronary artery disease. The habit of regular exercise saved my life.

I feel very fortunate to be alive and healthy today—so that I can encourage you to develop your own good health habits.

"Of one thing I am certain, the body is not the measure of healing – peace is the measure."

GEORGE MELTON

Healing: How does my body repair itself?

I have given my body many opportunities to practice healing. As I described in the introductory letter to this section, I fell off of a thirty foot cliff, severely tearing the muscle behind my left hip and collapsing at least one disc in my spine. In seventh grade, I broke my right wrist twice within four months. As a teenager, my knee developed a painful condition called *Osgood-Schlatters disease* from playing basketball. In my thirties, I severely tore my calf muscle trying to dunk a basketball without warming up. At the age of sixty-three, I broke my neck (C-5 vertebrae) body surfing in Kona Hawaii. (Do you remember the rigid neck brace I wore for five months?) In every case, my body managed to heal itself.

Other instances of pulls, strains, tears and tendinitis, which were debilitating from weeks to months, all eventually regained normal function. One classic case is *plantar fasciitis*, an extremely painful irritation of the connective tissue that runs between the toes and heel of the foot. As with so many injuries, it is caused by overuse and lack of flexibility. On more than one occasion, when I was ready to declare the condition permanent after months of heel pain, I would become aware that the condition was gone. The human body is truly remarkable in its ability to rejuvenate.

One factor that plays a role in healing is the general replacement cycle of body tissues. By one estimate, we replace a billion of our cells every hour. A few cell types on the surface our skin and interior lining of our digestive tract are sloughed off into the environment at an amazing rate – as many as 40,000 cells per minute! This equals over eight pounds of skin cells each year – the reason why as much as 75% of household dust may be composed of dead skin cells!

Cells lining our digestive tract are replaced as rapidly as every five days and skin cells every two to five weeks. Red blood cells are recycled in the spleen every four months. At the other extreme, some neurons of the cerebral cortex, lens cells of the eye, and muscle cells of the heart are thought to persist a lifetime. Many cells follow a more moderate replacement schedule, bones cells every ten years and muscle cells every fifteen, for example. The variation in renewal rate depends on the role of the cells in the body and their exposure to damage. Taken in total, as many as ninety percent of body cells are replaced every three to four years.

This makes me feel young—until I look in the mirror! Even though most of my cells have been replaced, changes in support structures produce the characteristic wrinkles and sags of aging.

Many body cells contain stored "suicide enzymes" that are released when it is time for them to be replaced. White blood cells then engulf and digest the cellular debris, cleaning up the spaces between remaining healthy cells.

Just as the social groups of primates depend on communication, so do the groups of cells that compose our body. Following injury, a cascade of events occurs, coordinated by signaling chemicals released by cells. In the first minutes, blood platelets initiate clotting and inflammation, then signal for white blood cells to rush to the area. Dilated blood vessels produce the familiar redness, warmth, and swelling that we find at the site of injury as the emergency response team is gathered.

Although designed to marshal resources, excessive inflammation can produce swelling and slow healing. To limit inflammation, the application of cold is usually recommended immediately following injury. After the initial response is concluded, brief applications of heat may speed the healing process. With both heat and cold, limit exposure to avoid skin damage.

During this inflammation stage, white blood cells engulf and digest dead and damaged cells as well as any bacteria that may have entered the site. They also release chemicals that stimulate the growth of new blood vessels and attract cells called fibroblasts. Fibroblasts lay down a protein (collagen) matrix to provide a structure for new cell growth. They also release chemicals that attract replacement cells to the area and stimulate their proliferation by cell division.

If enough tissue cells and matrix remain at the site of injury, regeneration of the original tissue begins. In several weeks, the site may be indistinguishable from the surrounding area. If complete regeneration is not possible, then repair mechanisms heal with the aid of scar tissue. Although pain and inflammation may be gone in days to weeks, complete healing may go on unnoticed for months to years.

A similarly coordinated sequence is initiated to battle illness. When pathogens (bacteria, viruses, or parasites) breach our outer defenses, white blood cells initiate a two-pronged attack. Some white cells are constantly inspecting the spaces between our body cells, looking for foreign invaders. When they find something that is "not self", they engulf and digest it, eventually dying in the process. Pus consists mostly of the remains of these white blood cells that have sacrificed themselves in battle.

Other white blood cells called lymphocytes recognize foreign molecules on the surface of pathogens and respond by producing chemicals called antibodies. Antibodies attach to the invaders, neutralizing them and signaling other white blood cells to engulf them. Some lymphocytes have the job of remembering the molecular structure on the surface of pathogens, allowing for a rapid response to subsequent invasions—what we call *immunity*.

Evolution has shaped an amazingly complex and sophisticated immune system for our protection. One recent study demonstrated a 23% boost in interleukin (a white blood cell secretion) when subjects viewed *photos* of sick people! Our security system is always on high alert. Most of the time, our response to illness is remarkably efficient and successful. There are exceptions.

As I have mentioned previously, our bodies are not perfect. We cannot always heal hereditary conditions or chronic diseases. In addition, our immune system sometimes fails to differentiate between our own cells and those of invaders, producing autoimmune diseases like multiple sclerosis, lupus, and arthritis. Sometimes environmental factors, health habits, and aging combine to produce body damage such as heart disease. And sometimes our immune system fails to recognize rogue cells from our own body—and we get a diagnosis of cancer.

Medical science is making strides in all of these areas. Yet even with the most advanced medical care and the best health habits, sooner or later your body will fail you.

Of course, I wish you a long and healthy life, but I want you to remember that healing does not always mean cure. Sometimes healing means peaceful acceptance. True healing may mean developing an outlook and philosophy that puts the trials of life into a larger context. This is where spiritual understanding becomes so valuable.

God, grant me the serenity to accept the things I cannot change,
Courage to change the things I can,
And wisdom to know the difference.   Reinhold Niebuhr

The second half of these writings deals with matters of the soul and spirit precisely because they are fundamental to total health and healing. We are not just our bodies. We are not just our minds. We are something more.

"This art of resting the mind and the power of dismissing from it all care and worry is probably one of the secrets of energy in our great men."

CAPTAIN J. A. HADFIELD

Stress: How does anxiety hurt my health?

Most humans will die in a different way than all other mammals—slow deterioration caused or accelerated by stress. A stressor is any event that disrupts homeostasis (the body's natural balance). Stress is the body's reaction to stressors. An occasional stress response is natural. Chronic stress in unnatural and damages our health.

You have probably heard of the *fight or flight response*. Evolution has provided us with this stress response to deal with emergencies, as when a lion chased us across the savannah. Under such conditions, the sympathetic nervous system releases epinephrine and norepinephrine (also called adrenaline and noradrenaline) which place the body in survival mode. Heartbeat, blood pressure, breathing, and muscle tension increase in preparation for action while nonessential functions like the digestive system and immune system are inhibited. In addition to epinephrine and norepinephrine, which act in seconds, the stress response is sustained by a longer lasting class of hormones called *glucocorticoids*.

Our fight or flight mechanisms are designed to last minutes, the length of a typical emergency situation. Our brain, however, treats psychological threats (like the fear that our boss will be displeased with our work) the same as it treats an encounter with a lion. This means that living in our modern world of traffic, multitasking, deadlines, and high volume social interaction can lead to chronic stress. Our body is constantly in survival mode, with glucocorticoids designed for short-term benefits now causing long-term damage.

Elevated levels of glucocorticoids (like cortisol) effect brain neurons, interfering with learning and memory while increasing anxiety. If you are constantly mobilizing energy, you do not store surplus energy and you fatigue more rapidly. You even run a higher risk of developing diabetes. Chronically elevated blood pressure damages the interiors of blood vessels and strains the heart. Repair of bones and other tissues is interrupted when our stress reaction reallocates resources.

Stress also affects reproductive organs. In females, the menstrual cycle can become irregular or even cease entirely while in males, sperm count and testosterone levels decline. In both sexes, chronic or repeated stress response can suppress the immune system, making you more susceptible to disease or making disease recovery more difficult.

These negative effects of stress are not automatic, but as is often the case, they interact with natural human variations. The most accurate thing we can say is that chronic stress increases your *chances* of these negative health consequences.

In one classic study of stress and heart disease, monkeys were allowed to form social groups until normal dominance hierarchies were established. Subordinate monkeys at the bottom of the hierarchy, who have little control of their social environment and few outlets when stressful events occur, were much more likely to develop atherosclerotic plaques in their arteries. The same occurred in other groups of monkeys where the dominance system was kept unstable with the frequent addition and subtraction of group members. In fact, monkeys who were struggling to maintain their position at the top of the ever-shifting hierarchy were much more likely to suffer heart attacks. In both studies, there was a direct correlation between social stress and artery plaque formation.

Stimulation of the sympathetic nervous system during stress has two contrasting effects on the digestive system. When the lion is chasing you, energy comes from immediate supplies in the muscles and liver. Digestion is not a priority, so peristalsis of the stomach and small intestines stops. Meanwhile, all of the waste in the large intestines is just dead weight, so the large intestines accelerate their contractions in an attempt to jettison the excess baggage. This is why gastrointestinal diseases like colitis and irritable bowel syndrome are the most common disorders resulting from chronic stress.

I could continue to chronicle the effects of stress from ulcers to memory loss, but I think you get the picture. The stress response is a positive adaptation to emergencies, but when the body pumps our stress hormones too often or too long, they damage health. If you want more details, Stanford professor of Biology and Neuroscience Robert Sapolsky has written a highly informative and readable book on the subject called *Why Zebras Don't Get Ulcers*.

I have never doubted the negative effects of stress on health. When my brother was killed by a drunk driver, my mother never fully recovered emotionally—and was dead herself within two years. These kinds of anecdotes are common, but I never completely understood the connection between stress and health until I retired from teaching.

I loved being a teacher. If I had it to do over, I would choose the same career. However, even with cooperative students and a supportive environment, I still found teaching to be stressful. Though I exercised, meditated, and maintained fairly decent health habits, I suffered from my share of health issues that I now see were clearly stress related.

Triggered by allergies, I always had at least a couple prolonged sinus infections every year that required antibiotic treatment. Throughout my career, I had heart palpitations that were always worrisome, at one point prompting me to wear a heart monitor to make sure they were not dangerous.

In the later years of my career, I suffered from irritable bowel syndrome and was also diagnosed with diverticulosis (pouches in the intestinal wall that are prone to infection). Following several bouts of diverticulitis (intestinal infections) requiring strong antibiotic treatment, my gastroenterologist was discussing the likelihood that surgery would be required to remove part of my large intestine.

Following a particularly stressful year, a blood clot formed in my main coronary artery, requiring angioplasty and stent placement.

Then I took early retirement.

In the seven years since I retired, I have not had one sinus infection requiring antibiotic treatment. My heart palpitations have stopped. My irritable bowel syndrome has disappeared, and I have not had one episode of diverticulitis requiring antibiotic treatment. I am absolutely amazed at my immune system's ability to fight disease when it is not inhibited by chronic stress. I don't even get colds or flu! (That sound you hear is me knocking on wood!)

I know it is unreasonable to expect to live a life without stress. The goal is somehow to moderate your stress to the point where it does not severely impact your health. Exercise, mental attitude, life pace, and regular stimulation of the parasympathetic nervous system—which triggers the relaxation response—are key. (I will have more to say about the relaxation response in the *Seek in Silence* essay.)

Life is good. Relax and enjoy the journey.

"Touch seems to be as essential as sunlight."

DIANE ACKERMAN

Touch: Why is massage so relaxing?

In 1957, psychologist Harry Harlow began a series of experiments on the psychological development of young rhesus monkeys. In one experiment, he separated monkeys from their mothers a few hours after birth and placed them in a room with two surrogate "mothers." One was made of soft terrycloth, but provided no food. The other was made of wire, but provided food from an inserted bottle. The monkeys spent significantly more time with the cloth mother. Harlow concluded that contact comfort provided by the cloth mother was more important to the developing monkey than the food provided by the other surrogate.

In times of stress, the young monkeys would cling to the cloth mother for comfort and security. If the cloth mother was removed from the room, the young monkeys would exhibit extreme stress behaviors including freezing up, crouching in a corner, rocking, screaming, and crying.

Many psychologists of the time believed that showing affection toward children was of no particular benefit and some thought it might even be harmful. Behaviorist John B. Watson warned parents, "When you are tempted to pet your child, remember that mother love is a dangerous instrument." Unbelievably, the concern was that expressing love to the child would cause them to be spoiled or weak. Of course, today we understand the importance of love and contact comfort for infants, and experiments like Harlow's would be considered cruel, even when performed on animals.

I can think of no more appropriate way to follow discussions of health, healing and stress than to talk about the benefits of human contact. Our physiological and psychological responses to touch are vital to our well-being, with roots in our ancient primate ancestry. Although we must always be cautious when extrapolating conclusions from other primates to humans, the importance of touch is validated by our intuition and experience. In a safe and appropriate context, most people enjoy a tender touch, a back scratch, or relaxing massage.

We know that exchanges of grooming behavior in our closest relatives evolved as a form of social bonding, a critical adaptation for the success of the primates. I hope you have had the opportunity to watch video of monkeys and apes grooming each other to gain a sense of how it promotes cohesion among group members. Research supports the idea that our species uses touch in similar ways, from handshakes to hugs, from patting a child on the head to patting a coworker on the back.

Touch is the earliest of the five senses to develop in the human embryo and the most developed at birth. Simply touching a baby's skin creates emotional and hormonal reactions known as the "limbic touch response." Touch releases growth hormones that stimulate development, decreases stress hormones that interfere with digestion and food absorption, and promotes immune system function.

One study in a poor region of Bogota, Columbia reduced infant mortality from 70% to 30% by implementing "kangaroo care" in which infants maintain constant skin-to-skin contact with the parent's chest. Another study conducted at the University of Miami showed that premature babies who received ten minutes of gentle massage three times a day gained 47% more weight and were released earlier from the hospital than preemies who did not receive massage.

Babies who are cuddled and hugged during feeding release the hormone oxytocin. This hormone promotes stronger attachment bonds with parents and increases feelings of security. Infants who lack sufficient touching start walking later, talking later, and reading later due to delayed development. In extreme cases, lack of touching can contribute to a life-threatening syndrome called "failure to thrive."

The benefits of touch do not end in childhood. A good hug in an adult slows heart rate and lowers blood pressure, and regular hugs provide a cardioprotective effect. Just as in infants, hugs in adults reduce stress hormones and improve immune system function. Oxytocin, the human bonding hormone, is released with hugs, supporting emotional well being and happiness. Hugging is a positive health intervention!

Similar studies have been done on more targeted forms of contact such as massage and therapeutic touch. In addition to the cardiovascular and immune system benefits already mentioned, massage reduces pain, increases blood circulation, and improves body flexibility. Therapeutic touch has been used to reduce symptoms of Alzheimer's disease such as restlessness, pacing, vocalizations, and tapping. Though deeply relaxing, massage actually heightens mental alertness and improves cognitive skills.

Massage therapists are first line healers, stimulating the body's own powers of rejuvenation by releasing tension. Headaches, neck pain, and back problems are often the result of stress reactions. In fact, experienced body workers can detect areas of chronic muscle contraction that lead to a host of debilitating symptoms. Releasing such blocks can be a first step to reducing pain and restoring vibrant health without the use of drugs.

The body operates best when it is relaxed, limber and supple. A skilled massage therapist can be is a powerful ally in the war on stress response.

If you have ever had a good massage, you don't need a list of health benefits to get you back on the table. Whether by a professional, a friend or a loved one, appropriate touching just feels good. As social animals, we are hard-wired to enjoy being touched. The health benefits are a nice bonus.

My mother and father were raised in the Midwest, members of families that were physically reserved. Despite all of their wonderful qualities, my parents were not touching people. In fact, I do not remember my parents ever hugging me as a child. As a result, I was so physically reserved as an adult that it was socially uncomfortable.

I felt that I was missing out on an important aspect of life—the ability to communicate my feelings to others through touch. I resolved to change, taking personal growth workshops to help me get past my inhibitions. Not only did I become a "hugger," comfortable with physical expressions of my feelings for others, but I went another step further to take massage classes. I developed a respect for massage and other forms of therapeutic touch as powerful healing arts.

Giving and receiving massage has helped me in times of stress, and has opened up a new world of personal enjoyment and satisfaction. I am so grateful that I pushed myself beyond my learned limits.

May you never lack for warm hugs and gentle touches.

III. Mind Wisdom

Dear Adam,

The range of human behavior has always confounded me. Our species is capable of heroic acts of altruism, inspirational works of artistic expression, and soaring achievements in science, engineering, and technology. Yet history also documents heart-wrenching acts of injustice, cruelty, war, and genocide. Such dichotomy has often left me asking, "Why do we behave this way?"

I was always the tallest—and skinniest—boy in my classes. I was also very quiet and shy, especially around girls. I remember a square dance activity we had in sixth grade. The thought of actually touching girls made my hands sweat profusely. Of course, realizing that my hands were sweaty only increased my anxiety. The activity that was supposed to be fun felt more like torture.

It didn't help in high school to have curly hair when the popular style was straight and slicked back. (We used to call it a "duck tail.") In addition, I was growing so fast that my pants were often short on me. Other kids would tease me by saying, "Are you waiting for a flood?" I always felt unattractive and self-conscious. My lack of social skills only compounded my discomfort.

I majored in psychology in college, hoping to graduate with an understanding of my own thoughts, feelings, and behaviors. Why was I terrified of public speaking? Why did I do things that I immediately regretted? Why did I feel so different from other people? Why was I so shy?

Psychology in mid-twentieth century left me sorely disappointed. It is a young science compared with the likes of biology, geology, or physics. Perhaps it is the sheer complexity of the subject matter, but even to this day, there is no unified theory of the human mind.

One problem in psychology has been the difficulty in observing the inner workings of the brain. Improvements in brain-probe and imaging technologies are just now allowing scientists to peek inside the "black box" of the brain to associate the activities of nerve cells with thoughts, feelings, and behaviors. Within your lifetime, psychology and neuroscience will collaborate to provide a more unified understanding.

Even though it could not answer all of my questions, I did learn some valuable things from psychology. For example, temperament theory helped me understand how I am different from most people—and allowed me to appreciate my unique personality. My improved understanding of others also made me a better teacher—and a more compassionate person.

In this section, I will share some of my favorite ideas about human behavior from various approaches in psychology.

With Love,
Grampy

"If the brain were so simple we could understand it, we would be so simple we couldn't."

LYALL WATSON

Brain: What's inside my head?

A thorough discussion of the brain is beyond the scope of these writings (and the capability of *my* brain!). Here is a brief summary of some aspects of brain organization and function.

An estimated 100 billion nerve cells called *neurons* perform the work of the brain, surrounded by an equal number of helpers called *glial cells* that provide nutrients, support, and insulation. As was discussed in an earlier essay, neurons pass their messages from one to another across microscopic gaps called *synapses*. Because each neuron has branched ends with multiple connection possibilities, there are approximately 100 trillion synaptic connections in the average 3-pound human brain. Although it represents only 2% of body weight, the brain receives 15% of cardiac output, consumes 20% of total body oxygen and uses 25% of total body glucose (energy).

Surprisingly, an infant's brain contains more neurons than it will have in adulthood, with part of development requiring a pruning of neurons and connections. Learning, memory, and skill development are usually acquired through the formation of new synaptic connections on existing neurons. Although it was commonly accepted that the brain could not grow after adulthood, recent evidence indicates that new neurons can be created in adults under certain circumstances, such as following injury. In addition, it has been shown that environmental stimulation can increase synaptic connections well into old age. Harmful events— such as trauma, drug use, or extreme stress— can destroy connections.

Because of the complexity of the human brain, our infancy and maturation are the longest in the animal kingdom. The commonly observed stages of human development are directly related to the time required to mature neurons and form appropriate synaptic connections between them. For example, language acquisition requires the functioning of certain brain regions that are not available during the first two years of life. At the other end of maturation, the frontal cortex, which is responsible for self-control and decision-making, may not be fully functional until the mid-twenties. The neurons in this region do not complete their growth and development, including formation of their insulating myelin sheath, until this time. This explains a great deal about the behavior and choices of teenagers and young adults!

One useful way of conceptualizing the brain is to divide it into three layers. Acknowledging our evolutionary past, the areas of the brain nearest the spinal cord are called the *primitive* or *reptilian brain*. They include the brain stem and cerebellum that regulate such basic body functions as breathing, heart rate, blood pressure, swallowing, digestion, and movement coordination. These survival functions are automatic and unconscious.

Above the brain stem (occupying the middle of the brain) is an area that is most highly evolved in mammals—the animals with the most complex emotions. Referred to as the *emotional brain*, the *mammalian brain*, or the *limbic system*, this area responds to the environment through both the autonomic nervous system and the endocrine (glandular) system. Circadian rhythms, hunger, thirst, temperature regulation, fight or flight response, relaxation response, aggression, maternal behaviors, mating behaviors and sexual response are all governed by the mammalian brain.

Surrounding the emotional brain is the analytical brain of the *cerebral cortex*, with perception areas dedicated to receiving and organizing sensory information (from eyes, ears, nose, skin, etc.) and motor areas that send signals to the voluntary muscles.

Other functions of the cortex include attention, consciousness, language, complex thought processes, decision-making, learning, and memory. In addition, its role in social interaction has caused primates and cetaceans (whales, dolphins, porpoises, etc.) to have the largest cerebral cortexes of all animals (relative to body size).

Scientists have documented complex social behavior in cetaceans, including sophisticated communications with clicks, whistles and other vocalizations. They recognize individuals within their group and develop strong social bonds. They even have been observed to behave altruistically toward companions (e.g. helping the injured to the surface to breath). This level of sociality requires a well developed cerebral cortex.

As mentioned in a previous essay, the size of the cortex in the 150 species of primates increases in proportion to the number of individuals in their typical social group. (The larger the group, the more cortex you need to keep track of everybody.) As the most social of all animals, the cerebral cortex of humans accounts for nearly 85% of our total brain mass.

The richness of our emotional life as human beings is due to the interaction of the cortex with the lower brain regions. Sensory perceptions and thoughts in the cortex stimulate impulses that are sent through millions of neuronal connections to the limbic system for appropriate emotional response. The limbic system then triggers behaviors. For example, feelings of attachment encourage caring behaviors; anger may produce an aggressive fight response; fear may produce a flight response, etc.

Unlike other animals, our consciousness monitors our emotional state and behavior options in relation to our physical and social environment, allowing us to be less rigidly controlled by instincts. While we must acknowledge the power of our emotions, the cortex provides us with choice in our reactions and behaviors.

Although we often think of the brain as the administrator of the body, it is part of a dynamic system. The brain is influenced by feedback from the body as well. For example, immune cells under attack secrete a hormone called interleukin 1 which can make you sleepy, change temperature regulation (fever), and increase pain sensitivity (body aches). All of this is the body's way of telling you to slow down and rest so that resources can be focused on fighting the infection.

Other common examples of the body's influence on the brain include the effects of testosterone on neurons that increase aggression, and the well-documented changes in female emotionality associated with fluctuating hormone levels during the menstrual cycle.

The brain can also be dramatically influenced by events external to the body. The *hippocampus* (a structure in the limbic system) is involved in memory formation and spatial navigation. Hormones that result from chronic stress (like long-term child abuse, incarceration, or combat) shrink the hippocampus, shriveling the neuron branches. This can produce measurable changes in function similar to Alzheimer's disease.

Another limbic structure, the *amygdala*, is central to the formation and storage of memories associated with emotional events. Emotional arousal stimulates the amygdala, which then strengthens memory formation. This powerful structure has direct connections to the nearby olfactory center, a fact that explains the ability of fragrances and odors to trigger strong memories. In cases of extreme fear or trauma, the amygdala can produce such vivid memories that they become the basis of chronic anxiety, panic attacks, or phobias.

Understanding the dynamic interaction of the brain and its surroundings emphasizes the need to support our children with a nurturing and trauma-free environment.

"Psychology keeps trying to vindicate human nature. History keeps undermining the effort."

MASON COOLEY

Psychology: What's going on inside my head?

In the early part of the twentieth century, psychology was dominated by the "theories" of Sigmund Freud. (Quotation marks because his ideas do not meet the scientific definition.) He imagined human behavior to be the result of an ongoing struggle between the Id (unconscious instinctual drives that seek pleasure), the Superego (moral internalization of parental conscience and societal rules), and the Ego (which attempts to mediate the struggle).

Freudian psychology emphasized sexual desire as the primary motivation of behavior. He thought that personality traits developed as a result of childhood experiences related to psychosexual stages of development. For example, trauma during his postulated anal stage might lead to a rigid and controlling personality as an adult.

In retrospect, Freud's ideas may reflect more on his own personal struggles and his creative imagination than they do on human behavior. The widespread acceptance of Freudian thought is a classic case of the human mind's ability to fit events into a preconceived framework. (Much as an astrologer or palm reader offers generalities and our creative mind inserts the events of our life into the provided framework.)

Some of Freud's ideas, however, related to unconscious motivations and psychological defense mechanisms (such as denial and repression) have proven useful. Yet even his other ideas that have little scientific support have had a large and ongoing influence on western culture.

Another influential psychological perspective from the last century was *behaviorism*, the idea that behaviors are shaped by rewards and punishments. Championed by B. F. Skinner, these ideas developed from the study of lab rats in carefully controlled experiments. Skinner thought that psychologists should focus on observable events rather than hypothesized mental processes.

Like Freudian psychology, Skinner's behaviorism has had a significant impact on western culture, particularly in the United States. During my teacher training, rewards and punishments were a focus in classroom management, used for motivating and shaping student behaviors. Many parents also incorporated behaviorism in their child rearing practices, particularly emphasizing praise as the reward of choice to encourage desired behaviors.

Certainly, rewards can influence behavior—that is why it is central to all forms of animal training. Human behavior is not exempt. In one psychology class, the students conspired to try a behaviorism experiment on their unsuspecting professor. Every time he moved to the right during his lecture, they slumped in their seats and looked bored; every time he moved to the left, they slowly perked-up and smiled at him. By the end of the lecture, he was standing on the far left side of the stage!

Skinner's failure was one of reductionism. Rewards and punishments do influence us, but they do not explain the full range and complexity of human behavior. Just ask any teacher how often they have students who refuse to cooperate even in the face of obvious rewards and punishments.

Partly as a reaction to the negative implications about human nature found in both Freudianism and behaviorism, new psychological approaches began to emerge in the 1960's.

One school of thought, called *cognitive psychology*, contrasted itself from behaviorism by recognizing beliefs, desires and motivations to be legitimate areas of scientific inquiry. At the same time, they sought scientific confirmation of these mental processes, not the blind acceptance of psychological mechanisms like those postulated by Freud. The mysteries of the "black box" were to be revealed by the scientific method, not the unconfirmed insights gleaned from a therapist's couch.

Humanistic psychology, with roots in existential thought, also developed as a reaction to Freudianism and behaviorism. Often described as a "third force" alternative, it was an attempt to bring a more holistic and positive approach to understanding human behavior. Theorists like Abraham Maslow, Carl Rogers and Rollo May emphasized free will and personal choice as concepts that distinguish our behaviors from those of animals. From this perspective, people are seen as innately good with the potential to respond to higher forms of motivation.

In Freud's approach, behavior might result from the expression of sexual desire, or the need to avoid the shame or guilt associated with sexual desire. For Skinner, behavior might result from the changes in brain wiring caused by a chocolate candy reward or the praise of an adult. Maslow, however, hypothesized that humans respond to a hierarchy of motivations with fulfillment at one level leading to the possibility of motivation at a higher level.

At the bottom of the hierarchy, humans are motivated by the physiological needs of survival. Clearly, if one's supply of oxygen is cut off, breathing instantly becomes the highest motivation for behavior! In another example, the desire for personal achievement or artistic expression probably takes a back seat if one does not have survival requirements such as water and food.

It may turn out that Maslow's need hierarchy is temperament-centric. That is, an individual's highest needs may depend on their personality style. (See the *Temperament* chapter.) Although a worthy

Hierarchy of Human Needs

Self-actualization:	Independent Choice and Action, Altruism, Creativity, Artistic Expression, Spontaneity
Esteem:	Self-esteem, Achievement, Goal Orientation, Respect by Others, Respect for Others
Love/Belonging:	Friendship, Family, Sexual Intimacy
Safety:	Security of Body, Health, Resources, Family. Freedom from Fear, Freedom from Insecurity
Physiological:	Breathing, Water, Food, Sex, Excretion, Sleep, Homeostasis, Freedom from Pain

---

attempt to categorize human motivation, the hierarchy of human needs may not account for human diversity. People differ in their psychological needs and behavioral tendencies as much as in their physical traits.

Paradoxically, underneath our genetically and culturally shaped differences lie core psychological patterns, universal in humans because of our shared evolutionary history. As our understanding of human motivation and behavior increases, the possibility of abuse increases—by corporations, government, media, and other entities. Already, personal data (web page viewings, credit card charges, personal demographics) is being used to tailor pop-up ads on personal computers, as well as phone and email solicitations. This marketing trend will become increasingly sophisticated.

Understanding the needs, wants, and tendencies of human beings creates the potential for manipulation of individuals for political power (neuropolitics) and monetary gain (neuromarketing). Awareness of our vulnerability and vigilance by individuals and groups will provide our only protection.

"We have to believe in free will. We've got no choice."

ISAAC SINGER

Behavior: Why do people act so strangely?

Although lacking a unifying theoretical framework, psychology and other social sciences are providing insight into human behavior. One of the most basic questions we can ask is, *Are humans fundamentally aggressive and competitive or kind and cooperative?* The answer is *yes*.

Evolution has programmed us for survival and reproduction. We are not consciously aware that many of our behaviors are influenced by the hard wiring of our neural networks, shaped by natural selection over millions of generations. I have already introduced the idea that our mating choices are influenced by subconscious preferences for genetic quality, group status, and resource access. Our tendencies toward competitive and cooperative behaviors are also part of our nature.

Competition is the foundation of evolution, and therefore the law of nature. Humans, like all animals, compete for the resources required for survival, compete for opportunities to pass on genes through mating, and compete to maximize opportunities for success of offspring. Most animals have evolved one of two competitive strategies for reproduction as outlined below:

Tournament Species	**Pair Bonding Species**
Males seek polygamous mating	Pairs monogamous for life
Low paternal investment	High levels of male parenting
High male aggressiveness	Low male aggressiveness
High male strength, size, weapons	Males-females similar size
Males selected by combat	Males selected by females
Females select for good genes	Females select for parenting
Few males do most reproduction	Few offspring per male

Several lines of evidence (sexual dimorphism, testes size, genetic imprinting, and behavioral observation) indicate that humans fall somewhere in the middle of the spectrum. While most western cultures espouse monogamy, our polygamous tendencies provide an inexhaustible resource for soap opera drama and tabloid journalism. Females compete for males with superior sperm, ample resources, and loyalty. Males compete for access to females with good genes, healthy bodies, and maternal skills. Both sexes have instincts to protect and provide for offspring, the bearers of the genetic torch.

Competing for resources and defending the family require a certain level of aggressiveness. Some scientists in the twentieth century argued that human aggression and violence was natural and inevitable. Fortunately, recent studies have added nuances to our understanding, allowing us to envision a more peaceful future for our species.

Yes, there is a genetic component to aggression, partly related to testosterone, with aggressive acts peaking around age twenty in males across cultures. A common arena for violence is male-male competition for females or the resources that attract them. Yet, contrary to earlier analysis, age-related testosterone levels by themselves are not a reliable predictor of aggressive behavior. A lack of impulse control because of the immature frontal cortex plays a more significant role.

This universal pattern of age-related aggression is moderated significantly across societies by cultural factors. *Child rearing practices, socioeconomics, and behavioral expectations are more significant variables in aggression than genetics and hormones.* Most people are not normally aggressive and avoid intentionally harming others or committing acts of violence. When violence does occur, it is usually triggered by stress, pain, fear, or frustration that overwhelms the cortical mechanisms of self-control.

In certain circumstances, cooperation can be an equally successful evolutionary strategy as competition. This is based on a concept called *reciprocal altruism*—"I'll help you today in exchange for your help tomorrow." This is a driving force in the sociality of primates, particularly apes and humans. For this strategy to enhance reproductive success, social groups must be stable (so those you help will be around to help you in the future), individuals must be easily recognized (so you know who owes you), and members must be smart (to keep track of the complex social interactions).

Reciprocal altruism works because the investment you make in another (to provide food, defend, build shelter, etc) is returned. Cooperating individuals enhanced their success beyond what their individual efforts could produce.

Of course, the optimal strategy is to get the help of others and then cheat by not returning the favor. If cheating becomes the norm, then the entire system collapses, so species have evolved keen cheat detection skills. Some scientists think this is a key component of our sociality—making sure that our contributions to others are returned appropriately.

Because they represent a serious threat to the success of members, social groups have developed many ways of dealing with cheaters. Part of gossip communication in a group deals with the building of reputations regarding who is trustworthy, who has cheated, and who may cheat in the future (i.e. violate group rules for sex or reciprocation). Systems of rewards (food sharing, grooming, friendship) and punishment (bad-mouthing, exclusion, violence) are used to reduce the incidence of cheating in the group. When groups get too large to successfully monitor and regulate cheaters by social rewards and punishments, they often split into smaller groups. (Or in the case of humans, develop laws enforced by secular or religious authority).

Resisting the temptation to cheat on one's companions (whether it involves sex, work energy, or resources) often involves the delay of gratification, a function of the frontal cortex. Studies have shown that if the reward for cheating is far off, it is relatively easy to choose to delay that gratification and wait for the social rewards of playing fair. By contrast, if the reward for cheating is immediate and the reward for following the rules is far off, the frontal cortex expends enormous amounts of energy in its struggle to make the choice to "do the right thing."

Interestingly, if the decision to cheat involves hurting a close friend or family member, then the limbic system is more involved than the frontal cortex. In other words, it becomes a highly emotional decision.

The evolutionary basis of cooperation in humans is supported by brain imaging technology showing the dopamine pleasure pathways "lighting up" during cooperation. Even though cheating may produce more economic rewards temporarily in the social group, our brain seems to know that cooperation is the best long-term strategy.

From an evolutionary standpoint, not only is it desirable to enhance one's own success with cooperation, but those that share your same genes. This is referred to as *kin selection*. We are particularly willing to help our close family members—and we expect them to return the favor. Thus, the human cortex has to be capable of keeping track not only of "Who owes me?" "Who do I owe?" and "Who might be cheating?", but the same information extended to entire families and kinship networks. (No wonder we got so smart!)

The interplay of aggressive, competitive behavior with kind, cooperative behavior in the people with whom we interact can be puzzling. Sometimes we just have to shake our head and accept that competing motivations make us behave strangely.

"Returning violence for violence multiplies violence, adding deeper darkness to a night already devoid of stars. Hate cannot drive out hate, only love can do that."

MARTIN LUTHER KING JR.

Violence: Why do people hurt each other?

History teaches us that aggression and violence are part of human nature. But studies of both humans and other primates have shed light on this aspect of our behavior, leaving us with cause for optimism.

Chimpanzees remember individuals who have harmed them and target them for aggression—even hours after the initial incident. They are hard-wired for retaliation, a mechanism that maintains the social order and protects them and their loved ones. Similar behaviors have been observed in many primate species. Interestingly, Japanese macaque monkeys harmed by a high-ranking group member are too fearful to retaliate directly. Instead, they retaliate by attacking a lower ranking relative of the offender.

Studies of humans find the same innate mechanisms at work. Subjects who were harmed—insulted, ridiculed, or harassed—were then given the opportunity for retaliation. Brain scans showed the same reward circuits activated as if they were getting a drink while thirsty or food while hungry. Between 1974 and 2000, over 60% of all school shootings in the US were motivated by revenge—often for bullying.

The ancient "eye for an eye" teaching of the Hebrew Bible clearly codifies a natural human tendency for revenge. The threat of retaliation has been a primary tool for controlling aggressive members of any social group. The good news is that we are also programmed for forgiveness.

Escalating rounds of retribution would have interfered with the social cooperation necessary for our ancestors' survival. Tolerating and excusing those we live and work with has always been necessary to maintain our social cohesion. Thankfully, the tendency for forgiveness is rooted just as deeply as our tendency for revenge. Societal living requires us to overlook the myriad shortcomings and transgressions of those that surround us.

We can reduce violence by recognizing our innate tendency for retribution while cultivating our equally innate tendency for forgiveness.

Much of the wisdom I will share on aggression and violence comes from a lecture series by Dr. Robert Sapolsky, a professor of neuroscience at Stanford University. He studied a troop of wild baboons in their natural environment over many years. After a tourist lodge was built in the area, the most aggressive and least socialized baboon males developed the habit of traveling over a mile every afternoon to scavenge the garbage produced by the lodge. Eventually, a disease spread from contaminated garbage, killing off all of the most aggressive males in the troop. The remaining troop, with only the least aggressive and socially affiliated males surviving, had an altogether different culture with a drastically reduced incidence of violence.

Fifteen years after this event, through the emergence of several new groups of adolescent males, levels of violence remained low. Not only that, but when young male baboons raised in more violent troops entered the group (baboon males typically change troops after puberty), their levels of violence were reduced to fit the new norm of this troop.

Dr.Franz Duvall of Emory University observed that various species of macaque monkeys differ markedly in their levels of violent behavior within their social group. If, however, you take infant monkeys from a violent species and allow them to be raised in the social group of a more peaceful species, they take on the behavior patterns of the less violent society.

The picture that emerges is that violence is amenable to social moderation.

Additional hopeful evidence was gathered by Dr. Harry Harlow of the University of Wisconsin. He demonstrated that monkeys raised without their mother to show them the rules become inappropriately aggressive adults. With normal parental training, the young monkeys grow up to be much less violent.

In these and other primate studies, there is evidence that nonviolence can be taught, that cultural norms can reduce levels of violence, and that nonviolence can be passed on multi-generationally. Evidence is accumulating that these observations in primates also apply to humans. Both scientific studies and casual observations offer us hope that we can break the cycle of violence by making positive changes in our culture. I will have more to say about this in *Living with Wisdom*.

The same mirror neurons (see next essay) that produce empathy in humans are hypothesized to increase violent behavior in people exposed to violence in childhood. Although sometimes labeled as controversial, the strength of the relationship between exposure to violence and aggressive behavior far exceeds the relationship between passive smoking and lung cancer, asbestos exposure and lung cancer, or calcium intake and bone mass.

Children can learn self-control and the appropriate contexts for aggression. They can also learn to be more violent. Even though most abused children do not become abusive adults, abused children have an increased likelihood for aggressive and violent behavior later in life. Observing violence (even on television, in movies, or in video games) does not create violent children. It does, however, increase violent acts in those who already *have* that tendency.

Charles Whitman was an altar boy and Eagle Scout. He also had an abusive father and dysfunctional family. On August 1, 1966, after brutally killing both his wife and mother, he took weapons to the top of the tower on the University of Texas campus and proceeded to kill 14 more people and wound 32. He was only stopped when fatally shot by police. An autopsy showed that he had a brain tumor that likely affected his hypothalamus and amygdala, the regulators of aggression.

What caused this horrific outburst of violence? Do we blame his childhood? his military training? his amphetamine use? his recent stress? his brain cancer? There is no answer because all could have played a role. Human behavior is too complex to be reduced to simple cause and effect relationships.

We do know that the amygdala plays a role in aggression and it seems reasonable in this case that brain disease may have made the difference between a disturbed young man and a mass murderer. Fortunately, such tumors are rare, but tumors are not the only thing that can sensitize the amygdala. It has many glucocorticoid receptors that make it highly influenced by stress hormones, which reduce the threshold for violence. It also has lots of receptors for testosterone which make males more likely to commit aggressive and violent acts than females.

Many studies show that the more a person is raised to "do the right thing" as a moral imperative, the more they will make moral and ethical choices as adults. With proper experience, it is as if the frontal cortex develops more staying power and moral action becomes a reflex.

A well-developed frontal cortex can control the amygdala. We have the power to reduce violence by the way we raise our children and by the cultural norms that we support in our attitudes and actions.

In September of 1848, Phineas Gage was the foreman of a crew cutting a railroad bed in Vermont. He was using a tamping iron (1.25 inches in diameter, 43 inches long) to pack explosives into a hole when the powder detonated. The thirteen-pound rod shot skyward, penetrating Gage's left cheek, destroying much of his frontal cortex, and exiting through the top of his skull. Though immediately blinded in his left eye, he remained lucid enough to tell the local doctor who treated him, "Here is business enough for you!"

Remarkably, his injuries healed, but the damage to his brain caused a complete personality change. He could no longer follow plans, uttered "the grossest profanity" and showed "little deference for his fellows." The railroad construction company refused to take him back and his friends found him "no longer Gage." John Harlow, a doctor that followed him during his recovery, said that the balance between his "intellectual faculties and animal propensities" was gone.

This case became famous in psychological literature because it demonstrated the role of the frontal cortex in decision-making and impulse control. Interestingly, there are some reports that Pheneas's behavior improved over time, but the accepted belief among doctors and scientists was that the brain was incapable of growth after childhood. (It would be another century and a half before technology would allow the gathering of evidence to the contrary.)

Violent sociopaths have less active frontal cortexes. Aggressive teenage males have immature frontal cortexes. Abused and neglected children have their frontal cortexes inhibited by hyperactive amygdales (damaged by stress hormones), sometimes increasing their tendency for adult violence. Alcohol inhibits the frontal cortex and can trigger violence in those predisposed. The pattern seems clear.

Humans are capable of inflicting great pain and suffering through violence. We are also capable of reducing violence through our concerted action:

- We can raise children in ways that develop active and trained frontal cortexes that allow for impulse control.
- We can prevent the trauma and chronic stress that reduces the threshold of the amygdala for the fight response.
- We can protect the rights of individuals and provide for personal security that does not depend on retaliation.
- We can create a fair and equitable society that reduces the levels of frustration and "no way out" feelings that stem from economic insecurity.

Of course, a society as large and impersonal as ours requires a criminal justice system, but our exploding prison population surely tells us that the solution to violence and crime does not lie in building more prisons. Rather, it lies in improved parenting skills and modeling during family life. It lies in education and opportunity. It lies in our conscious effort to create a culture of nonviolence.

Nonviolence flows naturally from compassion for our fellow human beings. Beneath our cultural differences and unique personalities lies our common humanity. I am inspired and heartened when I see the response of individuals and communities to each other in times of disaster. We need to nurture those feelings of interconnectedness. The more we focus on our brotherhood and sisterhood, the more we trigger our natural tendencies for cooperation, compassion and forgiveness.

Philo of Alexandria had some wise words:
Be kind, for everyone you meet is fighting a great battle.

"Life is just a mirror, and what you see out there, you must first see inside of you.

WALLY "FAMOUS" AMOS

Mirroring: What is the basis of empathy?

It may seem like common sense to say that much of learning occurs through imitation. Every parent has watched their child play dress-up and imitate adult behavior. How often do we hear people say things like, "You sound just like your mother when you say that" or "Your father does that the exact same way." In the last two decades, science has discovered brain structures that may explain imitative learning and many other aspects of human behavior—nerve cells called *mirror neurons*.

In the 1980's and 1990's, Giacomo Rizzolatti and his colleagues at the University of Parma, Italy, were studying the neurons of macaque monkeys. They were using technology that allows them to implant electrodes into the cortex of the monkey's brain and actually record the firings of individual neurons. In one experiment, they isolated a single neuron that fired when the monkey reached for a piece of food.

Then one day (so the story goes), a researcher was working in the lab between experiments when he reached for something— and the single monkey neuron that normally fired during the act of grasping began firing at the sight of someone *else* grasping. Years of carefully fine tuned experiments have shown that approximately ten percent of neurons in the monkey cortex have mirror properties. In other words, they fire during both action and the observation of the same action.

Although more difficult to study in humans for ethical reasons (planting electrodes in brains is risky), a variety of other imaging techniques support the idea of mirror neurons in humans.

So what is the significance of mirror neurons? Susan Blackmore argues in her book *The Meme Machine* that what distinguishes humans from other animals, even more than language, is our ability to imitate. Babies only minutes old can imitate gestures that they have obviously never seen before. Not only do babies like to imitate, they like *being* imitated. Such back and forth interplay between self and other may be one of the major factors in reinforcing the development of mirror neurons in a young brain.

Mirror neurons may play a central role in language acquisition. Research shows that the more opportunities a toddler has for imitation games, the more likely the child will be a fluent speaker a year or two later. Children who have the best skills at vocally mirroring non-words have the highest rates of vocabulary expansion. The motor hypothesis of speech perception suggests that we perceive other people's speech because our mirror neurons simulate what we hear as if *we* are talking—and then we interpret what *we* are saying!

Interestingly, numerous studies have shown that the areas of a baby's brain that contain the mirror neurons are stimulated by live actions more than they are by actions displayed on monitors. This alone provides convincing evidence that plopping your child in front of the TV is no substitute for parent–child interaction. The baby's brain knows the difference!

One subtlety of mirror neurons should be mentioned. The word "imitation" is often used in discussions of mirror neurons, but the word implies a rather conscious process of perception followed by action. The word "resonate" might convey a more accurate understanding of this unconscious process when small groups of neurons are tuned to fire under very specific conditions. The same neurons that fire when we catch a ball also fire when we watch someone else catch a ball. By watching, it is as if we are also playing the game in our mind.

The discovery of mirror neurons has much more significant implications for humans than merely the ability to learn to speak or perform motor skills. They play a key role in our social abilities—the development of both theory of mind and empathy.

The concept of theory of mind was discussed previously as one of the unique primate skills, vital to our sociality. When we observe the actions of others, mirror neurons allow us to simulate the same actions in our own mind. (This occurs effortlessly, automatically, and unconsciously.) Through experience, which has linked the mirror neurons into a neural network, we know what our intentions are when we perform those actions. It is, therefore, an easy step to infer the intentions of others when we observe them engaging in the same behaviors. Mirror neurons allow us to reenact the behaviors of others, giving us a clear understanding of their intentions and mental state—a theory of what is in their mind.

Several studies support this simulation model, demonstrating that mirror neurons are less concerned with the specific details of an action as with the goals of the action. For example, mirror neurons that fire when fingers grasp food to bring it to the mouth, do not fire when we grasp non-food. Nor do they fire when food is grasped but not brought to the mouth. Our mirror neurons are tuned to the understanding of goals and intentions, not the superficial elements of behaviors. Such understanding is essential in a social world where our survival and reproduction depends on our ability to monitor and predict the actions of others.

Who can we trust? Who will support us? Who is plotting against us? Mirror neurons provide a neuro-physiological explanation for complex forms of social cognition and interaction. By helping us recognize the actions of other people, mirror neurons also help us to identify the deepest motives behind those actions—and therefore the intentions and probable behaviors of others.

How do we know what another person is feeling? When we observe the facial features or behaviors of people expressing emotions, our mirror neurons fire as if we were experiencing the same emotions ourselves. We do not just categorize the emotions of others at an intellectual level—we literally "feel their pain." This is the basis of empathy, one of the strongest of human bonds.

People who are more empathetic and responsive to their fellow human beings have measurably more activity in the mirror systems for emotions. The same brain regions that are activated when we smell a disgusting odor are activated when we see another with the facial expressions of disgust. When we observe emotions in others, *our own facial muscles briefly form characteristic expression of that emotion*, which in turn allows us to interpret the emotion that we see. This is true down to the level of our involuntary pupil dilation.

In a clever experiment, subjects were much less efficient at detecting the emotions in observed faces when holding a pencil between their teeth—thus restricting their own facial movement. When free to mimic the observed expressions, they interpreted the emotions with accuracy. We don't need science experiments to understand this, we only need to look into the eyes of someone who is tearing up in emotional pain and then notice our own eyes.

Emotions are a window into past events and future intentions. Our ability to have empathy—to understand others at a feeling level—is one of our most important social skills. It not only strengthens the bonds between us, but it also provides us with insights into the potential behavior of others, making our world more predictable.

Human mirror neuron systems are essential for learning, language, sociality, and empathy—all fundamental aspects of our humanity. We are biologically wired by evolution to be deeply in tune and interconnected with one another.

"Everything that irritates us about others can lead us to an understanding of ourselves."

CARL JUNG

Personality: Why am I so different from most people?

You have likely noticed that other people are different from you. Personality traits show the same variation as physical features. Yet our tendency, when we observe someone else's behavior that is different from our own, is to label them "sick, bad, stupid, or crazy."

The end of the last sentence is borrowed from David Keirsey, author (along with Marilyn Bates) of *Please Understand Me*. This is one of the most influential books I have read. First, it helped me to understand, appreciate, and accept those with personality traits different from my own (just about everybody!). Second, it helped me understand myself.

> *"People are different in fundamental ways. They want different things; they have different motives, purposes, aims, values, needs, drives, impulses, urges. Nothing is more fundamental than that. They believe differently: they think, cognize, conceptualize, perceive, understand, comprehend and cogitate differently. And of course, manners of acting and emoting, governed as they are by wants and beliefs, follow suit and differ radically among people."* (Keirsey & Bates)

Dr. Keirsey's book is based on work by the famous psychologist Carl Jung who recognized fundamental differences between people on four parameters of personality. Isabella Myers increased the usefulness of Jung's concepts by developing a test (Myers-Briggs Type Indicator) which allows for easy identification of the traits in individuals.

Extroversion-Introversion

One parameter of preference that Jung noticed was along the continuum from extroversion to introversion. This should not be confused with a measure of self-confidence or shyness. Instead, it has to do with an individual's preference for energy renewal.

Extraverts (about 75% of the population) find interaction with people to be a source of energy. Sociability is a strength for them and they enjoy being with people and developing a breadth of relationships. Other characteristics include a tendency to focus on external happenings and to experience loneliness when they are not in contact with people.

Introverts have reverse characteristics. They often feel different from "normal" because they represent only one quarter of the population. While the extrovert is social, the introvert is territorial, desiring private places in both mind and environment. Social interaction is energy draining rather than renewing for an introvert, and they will recharge their batteries working quietly alone or pursuing activities that involve few or no other people.

This does not mean that introverts have poor social skills or dislike being with people. It means, rather, that they will find even pleasant social interaction to eventually be energy draining, requiring alone time to recharge. On the plus side, a relatively high percentage of the creatively gifted are introverts.

It is difficult for an extrovert to relate to the introvert's experience of feeling lonely in the midst of a crowd of people. It is equally difficult for an introvert to understand the extrovert's seemingly limitless drive for social interaction. The introvert's focus on internal reactions to events can give the appearance of disinterest or aloofness to an unaware extrovert, while the introvert may unjustifiably label an extrovert's extensive social connections as superficial.

Sensation – Intuition

Kiersey believes that differences on this parameter of personality produce the widest gulf between people. It has to do with the kind of information on which one most relies. The seventy-five percent of people who fall in the sensation end of the spectrum want, trust, and remember facts. They value the wisdom of past experience and focus on the actual rather than the hypothetical. Words like sensible, practical, realistic, and down to earth are apt descriptors of these folks who notice details and want to deal with the "what is" of the here and now.

The twenty-five percent of individuals on the other end of the spectrum prefer the big picture rather than the details. They focus on possibilities and a vision of the future, and are better at grasping generalities of the whole rather than the specifics. They are described with words like imaginative, ingenious, and visionary. The intuitive is more likely to have complex ideas come to them as a complete whole and they tend to move forward relying on inspiration rather than perspiration.

Thinking – Feeling

These two preferences deal with decision-making, and are about equally distributed in the population. Those with a preference for thinking are more comfortable with impersonal, objective judgments. They may be labeled as analytical and are sometimes criticized by feeling types for relying on logical arguments while disregarding the emotional components of decisions.

Those at the feeling end of the scale prefer value judgments based on emotions rather than pure logic. Thinking types may label them as fuzzy thinkers or soft-hearted, denigrating their decisions as irrational.

The thinking-feeling parameter is the only one that shows a slight sexual bias, with men being about ten percent more likely to take the thinking route to judgments while women show about a ten percent preference for reliance on feelings. Personal connection and harmony seem to be more relevant in the decisions of most women. It is unclear how much of this reflects cultural expectations.

It is worth emphasizing that thinking types can be just as emotionally sensitive as feeling types. The difference is that while feeling types may enjoy the experiencing and expressing of feelings, thinking types are more likely to find them uncomfortable or even embarrassing.

Judging-Perceiving

Although Jung's labels may not be as obvious here, the difference between these two preferences is straightforward. Judging (J) types prefer closure, often feeling uncomfortable until a decision is made, while perceiving (P) types prefer to keep their options open and fluid, sometimes feeling uncomfortable *after* a decision is made.

A *J* has a preference for planning and organizing and their motto might be "work before play" as they take deadlines seriously. A *P* is a direct opposite and can sometimes drive *J* types crazy with their general disregard for deadlines, and their tendency to move to new projects before old ones are complete.

Keep in mind that an individual's position on any of these four scales can vary in strength. In addition, mature personalities have the ability to express traits from both ends of the spectrum depending on context. Understanding the ways that you differ from others provides valuable insight, but natural preference does not have to mean limitation.

"I want freedom for the full expression of my personality."

MAHATMA GANDHI

Temperament: How can I better understand others?

Looking at the four parameters from the previous essay, it can be readily seen that there are sixteen possible combinations of the preferences. The first letters of the traits are often used to abbreviate these combinations (with "N" standing for "iNtuition" since "I" stands for "Introvert"). Thus, the combination of personality traits may be represented as ESFP, ENTP, ISFJ, etc. Each of the sixteen possibilities is called a *psychological type*; a particularly useful concept because each type will most often behave in predictable ways based on personality preferences.

I highly recommend that you take the Myers-Briggs Type Indicator test or the simpler Keirsey Temperament Sorter as found online or in *Please Understand Me*. Reading about the tendencies of your own type can be fascinating.

Learning and remembering the behavioral tendencies of the other fifteen types, however, may be a daunting task. Keirsey has offered a useful simplification, suggesting that four combinations of traits (SJ, SP, NF, NT) capture fundamental differences in human motivation. Keirsey calls these four major categories of personality *temperaments*.

Understanding the four temperaments can be very useful in interpersonal relationships. For me, insight into the primary motivations of others has made it easier to understand the behavior of others. Instead of labeling or judging, I can accept the differences between people for what they are—natural variation.

Here is an introduction to the four temperament types as described by Dr. Keirsey.

SJ – Guardians (Conscientious Helpers) ESTJ, ESFJ, ISTJ, ISFJ

The primary motivation for an SJ is establishing and maintaining strong social ties by being of service to others. Individuals with this temperament seek relatedness, belonging, acceptance, and appreciation from those they serve. Believing in the virtues of hard work and sacrifice, their efforts preserve our most important social institutions ranging from local schools and churches to corporations and government.

SJs usually like: knowing what is expected of them, doing a good job, stability and tradition, caring for and helping others. Words that describe them include: responsible, dependable, loyal, trustworthy, conforming, prepared, industrious, practical, dutiful, and devoted. It is appropriate to think of them as the pillars of society, the ones who can always be counted on, the glue that binds families and communities.

Representing around forty percent of the population, they are the largest of the temperament groups. If you think of someone who works hard without seeking recognition; someone who is willing to sacrifice to get the job done; someone who will not shirk the burdens of responsibility—you are probably thinking of an SJ.

Famous examples include George Washington, Harry Truman, Queen Elizabeth II, Florence Nightingale and Mother Teresa.

Good mental and physical health for a Guardian requires recognition of their tendency to take on too much. In their quest to be of service to others, they may become overwhelmed by their obligations. Not wanting to let down coworkers or family, they will work themselves to exhaustion and sickness. Although they would gladly sacrifice themselves for others, they must learn to set limits and maintain balance in their lives to be able to keep their primary commitments—and their health.

SP – Artisans (Impulsive Doers) ESTP, ESFP, ISTP, ISFP

The primary motivation for an SP is to act spontaneously on their impulses. Individuals with this temperament do not like to be bound, confined, or obligated. Doing as they want when they want is their primary goal. The most energetic of all the types, they can become skillful at sports or performing arts because they will "do" their favorite activities for hours on end (not for practice, but for the sheer pleasure of it).

SPs usually like: having exciting fun, being outdoors, trying new things, being absorbed in activities, and working with their hands. Words that describe them include: free, active, daring, adventuresome, independent, exciting, competitive, playful, physical, fun loving, and pleasure seeking. They learn best by doing, work well under pressure and are skilled at adapting to the demands of the moment.

Representing about one third of the population, they add spice to life with their enthusiasm and willingness to take risks. If you think of someone who would be key to a successful party; someone who stays in the here and now; someone who lives life to the fullest with a devil-may-care attitude—you are probably thinking of an SP.

Famous examples include Teddy Roosevelt, FD Roosevelt, John Kennedy, Amelia Earhart, and Ernest Hemingway.

Acting spontaneously on impulses may put an SP in conflict with social norms. The search for excitement may lead to rule breaking, even to the point of addiction or incarceration. The healthy SP must seek outlets for their need for activity, whether it is participating in sports, playing in a band, finding stimulating social interaction, or some other exciting pastime with manageable levels of risk. Career choices that take advantage of their people skills and their ability to work under pressure can add to the life satisfaction and mental health of the SP.

NF – Idealists (Meaning Seekers) ENFP, ENFJ, INFP, INFJ

The primary motivation for an NF is the search for meaning and personal growth. Individuals with this temperament seek identity and the expression of their full potential. Possessing an almost mystical ability to sense the feelings of others, they enjoy deep, meaningful relationships. Their empathetic understanding of people may combine with their creativity as a gift for poetry, literature, art or music.

NFs usually like: acceptance as themselves, intense relationships, self-understanding, self-expression, fairness, honesty, being unique, and having a purpose in life. Words that describe them include: emotional, romantic, idealistic, sensitive, dramatic, personal, suggestible, and imaginative. Often warm and well liked by others, they want to feel that their relationships and their work make a difference in the world.

Representing less than twenty percent of the population, their impact is greater than their numbers. Positive social change and spiritual development are usually led by their idealistic energy. If you think of someone who prefers to focus on possibilities rather than the details of reality; someone who is easily distracted and may daydream a lot; someone who will work passionately to right social injustice—you are probably thinking of an NF.

Famous examples include Martin Luther King, Jr., Mahatma Gandhi, Eleanor Roosevelt, Joan of Arc, Albert Schweitzer and Emily Dickinson.

NFs thrive in work environments where they are free to express their creativity and talent. Using their personal gifts to contribute to social harmony and the achievement of meaningful goals is deeply satisfying. To maintain mental health, an NF will do well to develop relationships with like-minded people who validate their individual uniqueness.

NT – Rationals (Logical Thinkers) ENTP, ENTJ, INTP, INTJ

The primary motivation for an NT is the improvement of their knowledge and skills. Individuals with this temperament seek to understand how the world works in order to be in control. They can appear unemotional to others because they do not express the depth of their feelings easily. Their lack of social skills and passion for learning can lead to them being labeled as "geeks" or "nerds". Just as the NF's often make major contributions to the arts, NT's have led the way in science and technology.

NTs usually like: mastery of complex knowledge or skills, technology, logical argument, excelling at what they do, figuring things out for themselves, and accomplishing goals. Words that describe them include: skeptical, analytical, rational, pragmatic, knowledgeable, skilled, ingenious, individualistic, self-critical, distant, and unemotional. If academically inclined, they can be gifted students in areas that interest them. Because of their drive to unlock the secrets of nature, they have done much to shape our understanding of the world.

Representing about ten percent of the population, they are a scarce resource that drives scientific and technological advancement. If you think of someone who is strong willed and loves analytical argument; someone who is an expert in their field of interest; someone who values intelligence and can be wholly absorbed in learning—you are probably thinking of an NT.

Famous examples include Thomas Jefferson, Dwight Eisenhower, Margaret Thatcher, Aristotle, Newton, Einstein, Charles Darwin, Marie Curie and Bill Gates.

An NT needs the support of people who understand that their lack of emotional expression does not mean a lack of feelings. They find deep satisfaction in interactions with others who share their interests and expertise, whether it is car repair, video games, or particle physics.

It is always dangerous to categorize people and then imagine that we completely understand them. This is the basis of stereotyping. On the other hand, realizing that variation in human personality is natural and that others are motivated by a variety of needs is a valuable insight. We can avoid condemning people who are different; instead recognizing and appreciating their gifts and talents.

Temperament and Psychological Type represent a model for understanding some aspects of human behavior. Other factors— like the levels of aggressiveness associated with prenatal testosterone exposure— also contribute to individual personality traits. At some point, I expect that these and other parameters of personality will be refined and associated with genetic precursors, increasing our understanding.

The more we learn, the more we will be able to accept the fact that human behavior shows great variation—eliminating the need to label others as sick, bad, stupid, or crazy.

"Sometimes the mind, for reasons we don't necessarily understand, just decides to go to the store for a quart of milk."

DIANE FROLOV

Mind: Why does my mind have a mind of its own?

Some years ago, I read a book titled *Multimind* by Robert Ornstein that completely shifted my understanding of how my mind works. These ideas fit my personal experience better than any other model of mind I had run across—and actually gave me some peace of mind! My personal experience had been that my mind was often in a tug–of–war, with desires battling self-control and thoughts battling feelings. Suddenly, it all made sense.

We have already seen how the mind is divided into three main regions that we may label as reptilian brain, mammalian brain and primate brain. You have probably also heard that the brain has a left (analytical) side and a right (intuitive) side. As convenient as these divisions are, Ornstein suggests that a more helpful representation may be that "stuck side by side, inside the skin, inside the skull, are several special purpose, separate, and specific small minds." Terms like *neural networks* or *mind modules* may be applied to these independent yet interconnected functional units.

The human mind is a product of evolution and, as always, we need to be cognizant of natural variation between individuals. We have multiple kinds of memories, multiple kinds of intelligence, and multiple kinds of talents. We each have a different combination of mind modules as unique as our facial features.

We do not operate as a single mind, but a coalition of many minds, each with its own responsibilities for enhancing our chances for survival and reproduction. This can be a difficult concept to grasp because we operate under the illusion that our mind is a unified and consistent whole.

Have you ever judged your own behavior after the fact and asked, "Why did I do that?" We usually come up with a reasonable rationalization, but it might be more helpful to realize that one of our many minds triggered that behavior for reasons we may never know. This is an unsettling proposition. For example, the "get enough calories to survive" module may be providing you with a craving for chocolate, while at the same time, the "look good to attract a mate" module may be insisting that you need to stop eating sweets to lose weight. Our mind modules have evolved with different priorities and may even operate at cross-purposes.

If we view our mind as a coalition made up of competing entities, a lot of our behavior begins to make more sense. Imagine a mind that can say both: "I know cigarette smoking causes cancer" and "I smoke". This kind of contradiction creates discomfort in any rational mind. Someone might say, "I will stop smoking before it can harm me" or "they will soon have a cure for cancer." Such rationalizations help us resolve the inconsistencies between thoughts and behavior.

One of my favorite concepts in introductory psychology is *cognitive dissonance*—one way our mind attempts to deal with the inconsistencies between its modules. For example, the more we pay for an item, the more likely we are to think it is of high quality. (The alternative is that we must have made a foolish choice!) If we work at a low-paying job, cognitive dissonance may cause us to report that we value other aspects of the job besides the income it generates. (Otherwise, why don't we quit!)

The way we understand others (and ourselves) is incomplete and misleading. We often use simple categories to label people, such as "nice," "aggressive," "selfish," or "thoughtful," as if their behavior was always consistent. When they behave in ways that violate our expectations, we are confused or disappointed. People are more complex than our simple labels because behavior originates in multiple mind modules.

In another attempt to find consistency where it does not exist, we tend to attribute our successes to internal dispositions and our failures to external circumstances. When Jimmy Carter won the presidency, it is reported that he attributed the success to his brilliance in organization, his skill in campaigning, and his personal drive. When he lost the election four years later, he blamed external events like a poor economy, energy crisis, and international problems. Blaming our circumstances (especially other people) seems to be a universal strategy for avoiding responsibility for our choices. This is not surprising when our multimind often makes choices we do not fully understand.

One of our brain's evolutionary legacies is an extreme sensitivity to recent information. Staying focused on our current situation was vital for our ancestors. Who cares about the lion that chased us yesterday when a poisonous snake is above our heads right now? Emotional upsets that completely engulf us quickly fade away when we change our focus. Our national interest in airline safety is intense in the days following a plane crash, but a week later, our attention shifts to new concerns.

Another survival skill of our mind is its ability to register only those things that represent drastic change. It filters the mass of input from our internal and external world down to the most relevant data for our well-being. In fact, we may experience only one trillionth of the information available to us.

Notice how news media attempt to counteract our natural tendency to filter by finding a "crisis" or "disaster" to catch our attention on a daily basis. They know that the potential for dramatic change is what people focus on. Newscasts often open with the most shocking or dramatic headlines even though the events are unlikely to really affect the viewer. The approach of a perfectly normal light rain puts the news team on "storm watch!"

These traits of our mind can slow problem solving and social change. For example, the news will focus on sensational murders that represent relatively rare events, while ongoing tragedies like death from hunger, disease, or drug abuse fade into the background. A murdered child will captivate national attention, while the 110 Americans (including many children) who die every day of alcohol related accidents is ignored—becoming part of normal background noise.

Our mind is also programmed to make judgments by comparison, which lead us to some interesting decisions. We will drive an extra fifteen minutes to buy soda on sale. We feel good about saving a dollar, ignoring the cost of gasoline or the value of our time. We think nothing of reducing the price of a house we are selling by $10,000 because it represents a small percentage of the total value, yet we balk at a garage sale when a customer wants to pay one dollar less than the price we have set (for an item we plan to throw away!).

All of these brain quirks demonstrate that evolution responds to the immediate survival and reproductive needs of individual organisms, not long-term goals. Our mind is the product of short-term adaptations across the millennia and we can see traces of our evolutionary past in the way our mind functions today.

To quote Dr. Ornstein, we have *"a mental system, comprising many diverse, even warring small minds, that seek to keep things simple and consistent, and it has brilliantly evolved a few major strategies to guide us through conditions that were appropriate for our ancestors. Unfortunately, these simple strategies, and our self-deception that we are whole, stable, rational thinkers, are often at the root of many personal, social and political problems."*

I will discuss some of the implications of our conflicting mind modules in the essay titled *Manage Your Multimind.*

IV. Soul Wisdom

Dear Adam,

When I was nine years old, mom signed me up for a Bible study class through my elementary school. One morning each week they bussed us to a local Protestant church, an old stone building decorated with creepy gargoyles and bloody crucifixes that frightened me to death.

Class met in the basement where the metal folding chairs were always freezing cold and the air was so dank, musty and thick it seemed to clog my nostrils. I thought there must be dead bodies buried under the floor.

The minister who taught the class was old and scary ugly, with huge clumps of hair coming out of his nose and ears. I thought he might live under the floor as well. The only things I remember learning are that I was a sinner, God was to be feared, and there was an excellent chance I was going to burn in hell.

My early fear of God was solidified in seventh grade. Our intermediate school was brand new and the playground was still dirt and rocks. Nevertheless, my friends and I would eat quickly so we could play football on the unforgiving field during our lunch recess.

Showing off my machismo I cursed, "God damn it" after a teammate fumbled the ball. The very next play, I fell on a rock and tore a big hole in my knee. My skin formed a scab and I didn't think much more about it.

During a game a few days later, I took the Lord's name in vain again. Bam, I fell again—and tore the scab right off my knee.

This time, as I looked down at the oozing blood, I made a connection. Was God punishing me? I told myself it might be a good idea to stop swearing, but a few days later the words slipped out again in the heat of battle—with the same result. I may be a slow learner, but three curses and three injuries were enough to convince me that God was listening.

One good thing I received from my elementary Bible class was a pocket New Testament. Following my seventh grade epiphany, I decided I ought to read it to increase my chances of staying out of hell. I have been on a path of spiritual exploration ever since.

Whether religion occupies a central place in your life will depend on your personality and experiences. Most people eventually adopt a belief system that is comfortable—and comforting—to them. We seem to need something.

Even though the majority of people accept beliefs from their culture without much examination, it is important to remember that belief is a choice. The following section explores a small sample of the options available to you. I hope you will find and embrace beliefs that are personally satisfying for you—and will help you contribute positively to the human community.

With Love,
Grampy

"The fairest thing we can experience is the mysterious...It was the experience of the mysterious that engendered religion."

Spirits: Why do we have religion?

In remote parts of New Guinea during World War II, some traditional tribal societies had their first extensive contact with technologically advanced cultures—the Japanese followed by the Americans. As you might expect, this came as quite a shock to the natives, and they assumed the newcomers must be spiritual beings with divine powers. They watched as the soldiers went about the business of building airports, which were soon the sources of all manner of wondrous cargo. They carefully observed the activities of the newcomers and often developed the belief that the cargo was undoubtedly a divine gift from their local deities or ancestors. Meant for them, it was unfairly being taken by the outsiders.

When the Americans left as quickly as they had arrived, tribal leaders convinced their followers that if they copied the activities and rituals of the Americans, the flow of the valuable cargo would resume to its rightful recipients. Anthropologists who returned to the island years later found that some tribes had cleared forest areas as mock airports, complete with control towers built of branches and airplanes made of straw. The members of the tribes had developed rituals such as painting their bodies with military style insignias, marching in drill formation with carved wooden rifles and talking on radios made of coconut shells. They did their best to copy the activities of the departed military personnel, with the expectation that this would soon attract cargo from the gods.

This was not an isolated incident. What have come to be called "cargo cults" developed independently in dozens of isolated Pacific Island cultures following first contact in both the 19th and 20th centuries.

Why do we have religion? Cargo cults demonstrate two likely features of a complex answer. First, humans have always invoked the supernatural as an explanatory principle for things they do not understand. In the absence of science, myths and supernatural beliefs developed to explain creation, death, celestial observations, weather and other environmental circumstances and events.

Second, lack of understanding led to erroneous connections—cause and effect relationships—between human actions and natural occurrences. We are predisposed to see misfortune as a social event, as someone's responsibility rather than the result of mechanical processes. In an attempt to control the uncontrollable aspects of their world, tribal societies evolved rituals and sacrifices they believed would influence the supernatural forces. Shamans were elevated as tribal members gifted in influencing the spirits.

Some scientists have speculated that religion may be a natural byproduct of our socially attuned brain. Members of our species are dependent on our social skills (reading the intentions of our companions) for survival and reproduction. We have developed this ability to such a high degree that we tend to see intention everywhere, even in physical objects and environmental events. (Have you ever talked to—or cursed—a car or computer to improve its performance?) This tendency to think of animals, plants, rocks, rivers, thunder, etc. as containing souls or spirits (animism) is nearly universal in the cultures of indigenous peoples.

Experiments have shown that children attribute motives (like, dislike, niceness, meanness) to inanimate objects such as triangles and squares that interact in a puppet show. Born as natural conspiracy theorists, we are always looking for the hidden motives and intentions of those around us. In the absence of knowledge, we apply those skills to the nonhuman world, attributing intentions to the physical objects and events that hold the key to our survival and success.

Many Native American tribes have, as part of their creation myth, a belief that large numbers of people initially populated the world, but then some transformed into animals. Because of this sense of shared human history, natives felt a close bond with animals, expressed through rituals that simulate animal behavior. Some of these rituals were used prior to hunting, with the intention of appeasing the animal's spirit so that it might be willing to be killed. These and other ceremonies usually involved drumming, dancing and chanting—a nearly universal aspect of the spiritual traditions of tribal societies around the world.

Drumming and dancing, chanting and singing, ritual and ceremony, all such shared experiences tend to bond social groups together. This feature of spiritual and religious traditions contributes to their staying power. Even as science has reduced the need for its supernatural explanatory function, religion has become more valuable as a contributor to the social bonding and stability of societies.

Physical evolution has supported these forms of social bonding by wiring them into our reward circuitry. Dancing, singing, ceremonies and other shared social activities release pleasure chemicals in the brain leading to reduced anxiety and increased feelings of well-being. Some research even supports the idea that religious tendencies themselves have a genetic component.

In most tribal societies, members react to the meeting of strangers from another tribe by either killing them or running away from them. There is no giving a "benefit of the doubt" or attempt at peaceful coexistence. The evolutionary driving force behind such behavior in a competitive world is obvious. As societies became more populous, many members of one's own group might be strangers. To maintain peaceful relations, rules of behavior had to be taught and enforced.

Moral precepts and rules of behavior are largely absent from tribal spiritual traditions. They were more concerned about controlling their physical environment than their social environment. Social rewards and punishments were sufficient to promote cooperation in a social group in which all members were well known to each other and remained in close contact. As populations grew, spiritual traditions became institutionalized into religions. Behavioral expectations were codified and partially enforced by the threat of supernatural rewards and punishments.

Religious moral codes usually have prohibitions designed to promote social stability—don't kill, don't steal, don't mess with another's wife, etc. This created a problem for leaders seeking conquest of their neighbor's territories. The highly institutionalized state religions solved this problem by interpreting their precepts as applying only to members of their own society. They avoided the uncomfortable cognitive dissonance associated with violating their own moral codes by arguing that theirs was the only true religion. The moral rules did not apply to actions against outsiders—those who believed differently. Unfortunately, it has been common for religious codes to be twisted by leaders and used as justification for war.

Anthropologists generally have not found fanaticism in tribal religions. But, like many institutions, as religion grew and became increasingly structured it also became more iatrogenic, that is, prone to produce unintended outcomes.

Religion helped make events like disease, death, drought, disasters, dreams and other disquieting events explicable (though my alliteration may be inexplicable). In addition, religious rules and rituals became increasingly vital for social stability as tribes became villages and villages became civilizations.

It is reasonable to ask, "Is there more to religion than explanatory myths and social bonding?" The next essays will have more to say about the development of religion.

"Look now how mortals are blaming the gods, for they say that evils come from us, but in fact they themselves have woes beyond their share because of their own follies." HOMER (750 BCE)

gods: Why are there so many different religions?

Except for some technological advances in areas such as tool making and metalworking, cultural evolution of our *Homo sapiens* ancestors was relatively slow for tens of thousands of years. Yet as far back as archeology allows us to see, humans have expressed a sense of the sacred. Supernatural memes developed and evolved locally, sometimes around concepts such as a powerful "Great Spirit," "Sky God," or "Sun God," but more often involving some broader forms of superstition and animism. Primitive temples and other sacred sites indicate that people were gathering for worship rituals even before the development of civilization.

There is some evidence that tribes living in bountiful environments developed complex spiritual practices, while those in harsh environments focused their time and energy on survival. (Maybe idle hands are *God's* playground!)

Around 10,000 BCE, human beings reached a cultural milestone which would change humanity and the face of the earth forever—agriculture. Domesticating crops and animals allowed humans to move away from the hunter-scavenger-gatherer lifestyle and (pun intended) put down roots. Consistent supplies of food energy allowed rapid population growth with villages becoming cities and cities forming states.

When agriculture was combined with irrigation methods in fertile river valleys, civilizations developed with large, highly organized societies, unified economic systems, wealth stratification, and monumental architecture. These cultural innovations also spurred the development of writing and mathematics for economic record keeping.

145

You may have heard of the Fertile Crescent (the Tigris-Euphrates river valley in the Middle East) where the earliest evidence of civilization dates to about 3500 BCE. Other river valley civilizations developed independently in Egypt (3,000 BCE), India (2,500 BCE) and China (2,000 BCE).

Ideas about divine forces in nature were common in early agricultural populations, particularly concerning animal fertility, weather and crop success. As civilizations developed, these ideas evolved into more structured forms of polytheism—the worship of multiple gods and goddesses. Ritual sacrifices, originally thought to replenish the abundance of nature, morphed into attempts to please the gods. Writing now formalized the mythology previously passed down only through oral tradition. Humanity lost some of the immediacy of its spiritual experience as religion took on more social and political roles in society.

Civilization allowed labor diversification, including the development of centralized government (usually justified by divine sanction). In many historic cultures, religious power intertwined with political power for the benefit of the ruling classes. Wealth and slavery provided the means for the building of temples, while ceremonies and rituals acquired increased importance in maintaining social unity. As feudal city-states came into conflict, they implored warrior gods for success in battle.

The growth of civilization sowed the seeds for a religious transformation that occurred nearly simultaneously in several regions of the world. Perhaps because not every waking moment was focused on the struggle for survival, an existential self-awareness developed. Some scholars have speculated that the rise of monetary economies and a growing middle class helped the spread of an altruistic ethic and egalitarian humanism. Concern for the welfare of individuals grew and, in an era of warring feudal states, ideals of a broader political and cultural unity emerged.

Every major religious tradition developed in societies racked by violence and warfare. *It seems that the main catalyst of religious evolution was the rejection of cruelty and aggression.* As an alternative, visionaries (philosophers, prophets, mystics and sages) promoted a spirituality based on nonviolence, respect, sympathy and universal concern. They argued that political peace and social justice required an abandonment of selfishness and the development of a spirituality of compassion.

Just as there occasionally have been the perfect conditions necessary for explosive bouts of biological evolution, so it has been for cultural evolution. The Renaissance, the Industrial Revolution and the Digital revolution easily come to mind. In this case, the social and cultural dynamics of growing civilizations created the conditions necessary for the emergence of the world's dominant religious traditions.

The German philosopher Karl Jaspers coined the term "Axial Age" to describe the years 800 BCE to 200 CE, which were "pivotal" in the development of most modern religions. "The spiritual foundations of humanity were laid simultaneously and independently…" The precursors seemed to have fallen in place that stimulated key thinkers in the Middle East, India, China and Greece—parallel developments without evidence of direct communication.

Here is a partial list of some of the philosophical and religious events of the Axial Age: (**All dates BCE**)

800 - 100 Sages in India compose many sacred writings including the Upanishads and Bhagavad Gita, part of a long history of oral & written tradition forming the roots of Hinduism.

800 - 500 Several authors write the Pentateuch, the first five books of the Hebrew Bible (Torah). Other Judaism prophets add books that eventually combine with the Pentateuch to form the Hebrew Bible (Old Testament).

628 - 551 Zoroaster lives in Persia. Zoroastrianism hints at monotheism, but also includes belief in two opposing spirits of good and evil whose conflict has created the history of the world. Individual souls are judged at death and sent to paradise or hell. These ideas later influence Judaism, Christianity and Islam.

599 - 500 Mahavira founds Jainism in India.
Lao Tse founds Taoism in China

563 - 483 Life of Buddha (Siddhartha Gautama). Born a prince in Northeast India, he renounces his life of privilege and seeks answers to the suffering of humankind through ascetic practices and meditation. After enlightenment, he emphasizes compassion as a way of life.

551 - 479 Confucius lives in China. Through wisdom sayings, he teaches the principles of a good society. Like Buddhism, Confucianism is more ethical philosophy than religion.

470 - 399 Socrates lives in Athens. The father of Greek moral philosophy, he becomes the teacher of Plato, who then teaches Aristotle. Although living in a polytheistic society, their moral idealism later influences Western culture through both Christian and secular thought.

460 - 450 Modern version of the Old Testament (Hebrew Bible) is compiled. Around 250, it is first translated into Greek.

4 BCE - 30 CE Jesus lives and teaches in Galilee and Judea.

70 - 100 CE New Testament Gospels are written, which form the foundation of Christianity.

Although the differences in the religions that developed in the Axial Age are notable, the similarities in core principles are even more remarkable. *At their essence, the major world religions all attempt to guide believers to compassion and altruism as opposed to competition and conflict.* They have taken sides in the battle between the two core aspects of human nature.

"Smoldering joy, oft-puffed by unceasing meditation, which blinded my tearful eyes, Burst into immortal flames of bliss...Thou art I, I am Thou, Knowing, Knower, Known, as One!" PARAMAHANSA YOGANANDA

Union: What do the Eastern religions believe?

The vast majority of people alive today (75%) are adherents of religions that have their roots in the Axial Age. Fully half of the human race claims one of the Abrahamic religions of the West— Christianity (2 billion), Islam (1.5 billion) and Judaism (15 million). Each of these religions traces their lineage to the patriarch Abraham—a sad irony considering the amount of conflict they have engaged in over the centuries.

Although expressing great diversity, there is an overriding theme within Western religious traditions. Christianity, Islam and Judaism all emphasize *laws*—rules for behavior given by God. If an individual follows the rules, they eventually earn the reward of dwelling with God in heaven. God is envisioned as demanding and judgmental on the one hand, but also compassionate and responsive on the other. Western religions emphasize prayer as a way of better understanding God's will and of eliciting God's intervention.

Other prominent Axial religions developed in the East, including Hinduism with an estimated 900 million followers, Buddhism with 375 million, and other traditional Chinese and Indian religions with over 50 million.

In Eastern religions, the goal is not to be in the same *place* as God (heaven), but to rejoin with God in an ultimate *union*. This is accomplished not just by following the rules, but by spiritual practices such as mediation which elevate the consciousness. Right action and compassion are practiced not to earn a reward, but as part of the process of lifting the soul toward its innate divinity— its true nature.

Hinduism

The primary ancient sacred texts of Hinduism are the *Vedas*, which developed in India as oral traditions before 1500 BCE. Formed of many diverse roots with no primary founder, the *Vedas* took written form in the Axial Age (800 BCE – 200 CE), with many other sacred texts like the *Upanishads* and *Bhagavad Gita* added during this time. Hinduism today is best characterized as a wide variety of religious expressions based on the Vedic tradition.

Contemporary Hinduism is primarily monotheistic, but Hindu tradition includes aspects that might be considered pantheistic and polytheistic. In one common form of this diverse religion, a single deity is recognized, with other gods and goddesses seen as facets, forms, manifestations or aspects of that supreme God. For example, *Brahma* the Creator, *Vishnu* the Preserver and *Shiva* the Destroyer are expressions of one God.

Hindus commonly believe in the *Transmigration of the Soul*, the transfer of one's soul into another body after death. This produces a continuous cycle of birth, life, death and rebirth, commonly called reincarnation. *Karma* is the accumulated sum of one's good and bad deeds, which determine how you will live your next life. In a caste system with strict social hierarchy, the unequal distribution of wealth, privilege and suffering were explained away as a natural consequence of one's actions in previous lives. (Clearly, this is a concept that adds to social stability in a society with such economic disparity.)

The main goal of life for a Hindu is liberation, a leaving of the karmic wheel of reincarnation and rejoining with God. There are several methods (*yogas*) which one can follow to achieve this spiritual goal: devotion, service, meditation, and wisdom. These increase good karma and lift one's consciousness toward realization of one's eternal union with God. In some traditions, God descends to Earth as an incarnation called an *Avatar* (such as Krishna) to guide humans towards Union—*Nirvana*.

Buddhism

Tradition holds that Siddhartha Gautama was born a prince in Northeast India (Nepal) around 563 BCE. Seeing the plight of the people outside the palace walls, he rejected the royal life and began a quest to find a spiritual solution to the suffering of humanity. At the age of 29, he left his wife and son and began the life of an ascetic, meditating and fasting to the point of near fatal starvation. At the age of 35, he entered into a meditation under a sacred fig tree (the Bodhi tree). After many days, he awakened to the ultimate nature of reality.

Thus liberated from the cycle of suffering and rebirth, he arose as the Buddha, a fully enlightened being. From this point forward, he lived in a state of Nirvana (extinguished, quieted, calmed) which is the goal of his followers. He spent the rest of his life traveling and teaching the path of awakening that he discovered. During his 80 years, Buddha attracted many followers who recorded his teachings and instituted monastic orders.

The first teachings of Buddha after attaining Nirvana are called The Four Noble Truths:

1. Life ultimately leads to suffering.
2. Suffering is caused by desire (craving).
3. Suffering ends when one eliminates delusion (ends desire).
4. Reaching liberation is achieved by following the Path.

The Eightfold Path to Nirvana includes:

- Right View (seeing reality, not the delusion of duality)
- Right Intention (renunciation of worldly aspirations)
- Right Speaking (truthful, without criticism or gossip)
- Right Action (compassionate, ethical, harmless behavior)
- Right Livelihood (support yourself harmlessly)
- Right Effort (work to improve, think good thoughts)
- Right Mindfulness (clear awareness with no cravings)
- Right Meditation (develop higher consciousness)

The spiritual practices of meditation and yoga are ancient in Eastern cultures, both designed to empty the mind and allow spiritual insight. Buddha emphasized to his disciples that they must not accept anybody's teaching, even his own, if it did not fit with their own experience.

In order to insure that he was fully aware of his own experience, Buddha developed the practice of *mindfulness*—staying fully conscious of the workings of his mind and body. This allowed him to combat the destructive tendencies of desire and to replace negative thoughts with positive. For example, it was not enough for him merely to avoid aggression. He sought to actively cultivate thoughts of loving-kindness and actions of generosity and compassion.

Although raised in a Hindu culture, Buddha refused to speculate on theories about the creation of the world or the existence of God. He told his disciples that such questions, "…will not help you, they are not useful in the quest for holiness; they do not lead to peace and to the direct knowledge of Nirvana." He considered speculation about an ineffable God to be distractions from the Path.

Hinduism and Buddhism, both with roots in India, embody a turning point in religious thought—external ritual was no longer as important as rigorous introspection. The worshiper was instructed to look within for the highest understanding of ultimate reality, which would lead to compassionate and caring actions.

Other Eastern Religions and Philosophies

The scope of these writings does not allow a discussion of Confucianism, Taoism, and other traditional Chinese philosophies that also emerged in response to the horrors of constant warfare. Each contains valuable insights into the reduction of human suffering and the improvement of humanity. The wide variety of Eastern traditions offers much to explore.

"If only God would give me a clear sign! Like making a large deposit in my name in a Swiss bank.

WOODY ALLEN

Law: How are Western religions related to each other?

Judaism

Most likely, the early Hebrews were pagans who shared many of the religious beliefs of their polytheistic neighbors after migrating to Canaan (modern Israel) from Mesopotamia around 2000 BCE. The Bible names Abraham as the founding patriarch of the Hebrews and one of his gods was *El*, the High God of the Canaanites. In Genesis 17:1, God introduces himself to Abraham as *El Shaddai* (El of the Mountain, one of El's traditional titles). The name of the Canaanite High God is preserved in such Hebrew names as *Isra-El* and *Ishma-El*.

People adopt particular conceptions of God because it works for them, not because it has a sound scientific or philosophical basis. In a region beset with near constant warfare and subjugation by foreign powers, the Israelite tribes gradually changed the Canaanite God *El* into the Jewish God *Yahweh Sabaoth*, the God of Armies. As a tribal deity, he is passionately partisan, a savage and murderous God of war—a God that the Israelites came to rely on for survival.

The pagan world was full of gods who could be perceived unexpectedly at any time in the environment. Because the divine was not distinct from nature or humanity, such epiphanies (manifestations of a divine being) were not considered that unusual. Thus, God reveals Himself and His expectations to the Hebrew people over centuries of interactions with the patriarchs and prophets. To modern readers, the idea of talking directly with God seems a bit unbelievable, shocking, or even blasphemous, but we have to keep the cultural context of the Israelites in mind.

The Bible recounts the history of the Israelites and their interactions with Yahweh, and forms the foundation of the religion of Judaism. Monotheism stems from a key concept of Judaism, the Divine Covenant. In essence, God makes a deal with the Israelites, agreeing to provide for them and protect them from their enemies in exchange for their exclusive devotion. Jews become the "chosen people" as a result of this contract with the one true God. (This does not imply that Jews are better than other people, only that they have a special relationship with God that includes challenging responsibilities and punishments for failure.)

The Bible tells the story of one of the pivotal moments in Jewish history when the covenant with God is reaffirmed. Jacob, the grandson of Abraham, leads the Israelites out of Canaan during a famine to settle in Egypt. Their descendants, enslaved by the Pharaoh, spend four hundred years in bondage. Yahweh selects Moses to lead his chosen people on a miraculous emigration out of Egypt and then gives Moses the Ten Commandments and other instructions. This marks the beginning of Judaism. Although capable of compassion, Yahweh is depicted as judgmental and demanding, and Judaism is a religion of Laws.

The first five books of the Bible (Pentateuch), called the Books of Moses, comprise the Torah, the most sacred of the Jewish texts. By following the commandments and laws in the Torah and other sacred texts, Jews believe their lives are sanctified and they can draw closer to God.

Yahweh is a righteous God. He knows the thoughts and deeds of His people and will reward the good and punish the evil. At some time in the future, God will send the Messiah who will gather Jews back to the land of Israel, even resurrecting the dead.

By adopting (or being adopted by) the One Eternal God, Judaism moved away from the gods of animism and polytheism and set the stage for the other major monotheistic religions that thrive today, Christianity and Islam.

Islam

Although technically outside the date range that Jaspers uses to define the Axial Age, Muhammad is a prophet who follows the classic axial pattern. A successful merchant, he lived in the city of Mecca that had grown rich as a center of trade and finance. The old pagan faith, which had served the desert dwellers well in the nomadic days, no longer seemed to fit their new circumstances. Old tribal values, such as taking care of the weaker clan members, had faded in the rush to wealth. Like so many of the sages and prophets before him, he found himself living in a society caught up in vicious cycles of tribal warfare and violence.

In 610 CE, when Muhammad was forty years old, he proclaimed that he was visited by the Angel Gabriel, who brought him revelations from *Allah*. By this time, many Arabs had come to believe that Allah, the High God in their pantheon, was the same God that was worshiped by the Jews and Christians (who they interacted with on their trading routes). For the next twenty-three years until his death in 632, the revelations were collected in oral and written form, eventually being assembled into a single book called the *Qur'an*. Muslims believe that Allah is the one true God and that the Qur'an contains the literal words of Allah.

Islam is the religion of Muslims. Muslims view Muhammad as the last and greatest in a line of prophets that include Adam, Abraham, Moses, Jesus and others who inspired the Bible. In the Qur'an, God instructs the Muslims to treat the "people of the earlier revelation" with respect and courtesy. Islamic tradition holds that the Bible, including the New Testament, reflects an unfolding revelation by God, but that it has been corrupted over the ages. This unfaithful interpretation of the Bible necessitated the giving of the Qur'an to Muhammad to correct the distortions.

Islam means "surrender" (to the will of God). When Muhammad asked his followers to prostrate themselves in prayer several times a day, it was difficult for Arabs who thought it degrading to grovel on the ground like slaves. Nevertheless, the posture was designed to teach them to humble the ego, which "prances, preens and postures to draw attention to itself." Muslims were also required to exemplify the virtues of compassion and generosity, giving to the poor and appreciating the bounty that Allah had given them. Followers were tasked with the responsibility to cultivate a caring and responsible spirit and turn away from selfish barbarism.

The most successful Meccan families rejected this egalitarian ethic, persecuting the Muslims and attempting to assassinate its prophet. Muhammad and seventy Muslim families were forced to flee to Medina where they endured a five-year war with Mecca.

During this dark time, some revelations of the Qur'an instructed the Muslims about their conduct on the battlefield. It condemned war as "an awesome evil" and forbade Muslims to initiate hostilities. Fighting might be necessary, but only in self-defense and only in proportion to the aggression of the enemy. Muhammad was eventually able to stop the war with a daring policy of forgiveness and nonviolence.

Islam carries on Abrahamic concepts including virtuous living, a judgment day, resurrection of the dead, and paradise and hell.

The most important Muslim beliefs are The Five Pillars:
1. There is one God, and Muhammad is His Messenger.
2. Pray five times a day facing Mecca (to focus the mind on God).
3. Fast during the month of Ramadan (to express gratitude).
4. Give to the needy in proportion to your wealth.
5. Make a pilgrimage to Mecca at least once in your life.

"I like your Christ, I do not like your Christians. Your Christians are so unlike your Christ."

MAHATMA GANDHI

Christianity: How did Jesus start a religion?

As the largest religion in the world and the wellspring of my own spiritual quest, I will focus added attention on Christianity.

In the early part of the first century CE, Judaism was composed of about two dozen competing factions, most with charismatic leaders and all following common Jewish practices such as observing dietary restrictions, worshiping at the Jerusalem Temple, sacrificing animals and observing the weekly Sabbath.

During this time, Judea was under harsh Roman rule. In response to Roman oppression, several of the Jewish sects taught an apocalyptic vision of an imminent end to the evil age in which they were living. These beliefs often involved a messiah, an expected king and deliverer, who would remove the Romans and establish God's justice and righteousness in the world.

In this unsettled environment, Yeshua of Nazareth (translated as Jesus, approx. 4 BCE—30 CE) became one of many wandering teachers and faith healers. He taught that the new kingdom on earth would not result from violence and warfare, but from a return to Jewish principles and a change in people's hearts.

The writers of the Gospels seem to indicate that Jesus may have started as a disciple of John the Baptist who preached against a hopelessly corrupt Jerusalem establishment. John urged the populace to prepare for the new kingdom by repenting and accepting the rite of baptism (ritual purification) in the River Jordan. Some scholars argue that Jesus was a Pharisee because his teachings closely matched those of the esteemed Rabbi Hillel the Elder who had lived a couple generations before Jesus.

Jesus (and other activist Jewish leaders who gathered large followings) made the Roman authorities nervous. Apparently as a result of his attack on merchants that he felt were defiling the Temple, Jesus was charged with insurrection. This was one of two crimes (the other was treason) under Roman law that carried the penalty of crucifixion. We can imagine the horror and disbelief that his followers must have felt when their leader, the man that they thought was on a mission from God, was torturously killed.

Jesus' impact on his followers did not die with him. His disciples and other followers initially fled to Galilee, but later returned to Jerusalem under the leadership of James, one of the brothers of Jesus. They thought of themselves as a reform movement within Judaism, forming a synagogue and continuing to follow Jewish laws and traditions. Many in the group had been close to Jesus; others had not known him but were inspired by his teachings. Some still believed he was the Jewish Messiah, others viewed him as a revered prophet and rabbi, but none saw him as a deity. As they attempted to make sense out of the death of Jesus, stories of his life were told and retold. Some of his words were eventually put down in writing. This was the beginning of what historians call the Jewish Christian movement.

Saul, a Jew from Tarsus, prosecuted Jewish Christians on behalf of the priests at the Jerusalem Temple. He experienced a powerful religious conversion, changed his name to Paul, and became the single most active missionary for Christianity. Traveling the Roman roads throughout the Eastern Mediterranean, Paul spread the stories of Jesus to Gentile (non-Jewish) groups, abandoning most of the Jewish behavioral rules that Jesus and his disciples had followed during his ministry. He developed the concept of Jesus as a "god-man", the savior of humanity, who was executed, resurrected and ascended into heaven. These stories were reminiscent of god-man stories in the established pagan and mystery religions that ranged from India to Egypt.

Scholars have pointed out that many of the beliefs and rituals established in Paul's early churches are remarkably similar to those of pagan hero/saviors that arose centuries before Jesus. The birth of Attis, the god-man of Asia Minor, was celebrated on December 25th during the festival of the winter solstice. Attis died on March 23 and was resurrected on March 25th, the exact dates that were used by the early Christians for the death and resurrection of Jesus. These dates also correspond with springtime fertility celebrations common in pagan societies. (Have you ever wondered about Easter eggs and Easter bunnies?) Whether Paul intentionally created these similarities to "sell" his new religion or whether they developed independently in the new congregations is unknown, but it is clear that many pagan ideas and practices wove their way into the Christian story.

Paul established many churches in urban centers throughout the Mediterranean region, which usually met in member's homes with no dedicated church buildings and no central authority. Much of our knowledge about the early church comes from letters that Paul wrote to the various congregations, answering their questions and trying to squelch ideas that did not fit into his theology. He preached the imminent arrival of God's Kingdom on Earth and salvation for those who converted to follow Jesus as the Christ (Messiah). He essentially was saying that God's covenant with the Jews has been supplanted by a new covenant with Christians.

The Jewish Christian movement in Jerusalem did not agree with all of Paul's interpretations of Jesus' message. It had a particular issue with Paul's Christians not following Jewish traditions, including circumcision. Paul went to Jerusalem to meet with the movement leaders including James, Peter and John. They reached a compromise that did not require Gentiles to be circumcised to be Christians. (Undoubtedly a boon to recruiting!)

Another movement called Gnostic Christianity also developed which had roots in a variety of pre-Christian religions and philosophies. They claimed to have secret knowledge about God and humanity and had novel interpretations of the Hebrew Scriptures and other sacred writings. After initially expanding to play a prominent role in early Christianity, they faded due to systematic persecution and extermination by Pauline Christians.

Meanwhile, Jewish Christians were killed, enslaved or scattered during two Jewish revolts against the Roman Empire in 70 CE and 135 CE. This effectively ended the Jewish Christian movement. Even though Paul was taken to Rome and executed in about 65 CE, his branch of the church survived and flourished. With no central authority, each community developed its own doctrines and interpretation of theology.

Eventually, a hierarchical structure evolved with individual congregational leaders recognizing the authority of a local bishop. This organization, however, remained decentralized with no person or group speaking for the entire church as a whole. Keep in mind that all of this took place under Roman rule with fluctuating levels of persecution. Congregations kept a low profile and organization remained regional.

Christianity received an enormous boost in 312 when Emperor Constantine had a vision that led to his conversion to Christianity. He legalized and supported Christianity, making it the state religion. By this time, more than forty different gospels had been written with wide variations in theological doctrine. The nature of Jesus' relationship to God continued to be one of the major issues. In 325, Emperor Constantine gathered bishops from the various regions in the *Council of Nicaea* to attempt a unification of doctrine, but the gathering achieved only partial success.

For two thousand years, the history of Christianity has documented people's attempts to understand the meaning of the life of a man called Jesus.

> **"A God that can be understood is no God. Who can explain the Infinite in words?"**
>
> W. SUMMERSET MAUGHAM

Bibles: Who wrote the Western Scriptures?

Following the Reformation, conservative churches began to insist that the Bible was the inerrant word of God, but archeologists and scholars have pieced together a history of the Bible that illuminates its human origins. This does not necessarily detract from the Bible as inspirational writing, but instead allows for a more complete understanding.

The oldest texts of the Bible appear to come from the eleventh or tenth century BCE. War songs such as Exodus 15 and Judges 5 celebrate Israelite victories that preceded the monarchies of David and Solomon. Most of the Biblical texts, however, are from more recently penned sources that have been artistically woven together.

The first five books of the Bible (Pentateuch), which form the Torah of Judaism, are often called the "Books of Moses" because tradition holds that they were given to Moses directly by God. Biblical scholars, however, generally agree that four authors and several editors were involved over a period of centuries beginning before 800 BCE.

One early writer is called "J" because he refers to God as Yahweh, which is often translated as "Jehovah." He was writing from the southern Kingdom of Judea in a time when the tribes of Israelites were split into two kingdoms. One revolutionary concept from J is the idea that man is not made of the same divine stuff as the gods. He created a pun when he wrote that the first man *Adam* was made from earth—*Adamah*.

Another writer uses the more formal divine title "Elohim" for God and is therefore called "E". He was writing in the northern Kingdom of Israel in a style that is more elaborate and sophisticated than J.

161

The author of several books including Deuteronomy (therefore called "D") probably worked from more ancient texts in about 621 BCE. He is concerned with the history of the Hebrew tribes through their various periods of trial and redemption as well as the commandments (603 beyond the famous 10!) that God had given the Israelites.

Another author is called "P" because he emphasizes the role of the Jewish priesthood. The author of P was probably a priest descended from Aaron, the brother of Moses, since he sets up Aaron and his heirs as the only priests divinely sanctioned to offer sacrifice. He views God as distant and less personal than J and E. P's most famous contribution is the account of creation in the first chapter of Genesis. He drew upon the *Enuma Elish,* the epic Babylonian account of the six days of the world's creation that was chanted during their New Year Festival.

The E document was probably carried south to Jerusalem and merged with the J material in about 650 BCE. Precise dates are uncertain, but the D material may have been added around 550 BCE. P was likely incorporated around the time that the Pentateuch took its final form in 450 BCE. Repetitions and inconsistencies that remain in the Pentateuch are a tribute to the editor's respect for Scripture. They were reluctant to delete or reshape sacred material, so the process became a devotional struggle to comprehend, organize and convey the divine message.

The other nineteen books of the Hebrew Bible are grouped into the Prophets (Joshua, Samuel, Isaiah, etc.) and the Writings (Psalms, Proverbs, Chronicles, etc.). The Abrahamic religions of Judaism and Christianity (and to some extent Islam) share much of the Bible as their sacred text, although with slightly different organization. The Hebrew Scriptures consist of 24 books. The Protestant Old Testament contains the 24 books of the Hebrew Scriptures divided and rearranged to make 39 books. The Roman Catholic Old Testament adds additional books for a total of 46.

Early Hebrew texts show remnants of polytheism, but the belief in monotheism was clearly established in the Axial Age. Deut 6:4 *Hear, O Israel: The LORD is our God, the LORD alone. You shall love the LORD your God with all your heart, and with all your soul, and with all your strength.* Yahweh is a jealous God. Only loyalty to Him will bring the blessings of peace, protection and prosperity. The Hebrew Prophets also implore the Israelites to discover that God wants compassion from them rather than ritual sacrifice.

One interesting concept that has developed in Judaism is that the Sacred Texts only come alive through study and discussion. Holiness is not the result of simple rule following. It results from consideration and application of the rules in the current situation.

Most Christian denominations add 27 books to the Bible to tell the story of Jesus—The New Testament. (Some Eastern and African denominations add a few more books.) Perhaps because the disciples (and later Paul) expected the imminent return of Jesus, there were no written accounts made immediately about his life. Focused mostly on his teachings, the New Testament was written from 20-70 years after Jesus' execution in 30 CE.

Our earliest writings are the Epistles (letters) of Paul which he began writing after 50 CE. These letters to fledgling Christian congregations like the Thessalonians, Galatians, Corinthians and Philippians attempt to boost their morale and answer questions, particularly about the eagerly awaited Second Coming of Christ and Last Judgment. The letters provide a vivid picture of the emerging Gentile Church that Paul and others were establishing.

At about the same time that Paul was writing his letters, some Christians began writing down collections of Jesus' teachings that had been faithfully kept in oral tradition. The best known of these collections is designated *Q* for *Quelle*, a German word for "source." All of the Gospel writers seem to have relied on this and other documents which are now lost.

The first written Gospel ("good news") is Mark, most likely written about 70 CE by someone not native to Palestine who was writing for a Gentile audience. The earliest version of Mark's Gospel contains no reference to Jesus' birth or his appearances to his followers after his resurrection. A second-century writer drew on later Gospels and the Acts of the Apostles to compose a new, longer ending to Mark that brought it more in line with the other Gospels.

Mark's Gospel was copied and disseminated among the scattered churches of the early Jesus movement, inspiring others to write their own accounts of the life of Jesus. Matthew and Luke (produced by unknown writers about 85 CE) were two that expanded on Mark's narrative. Because of their similarities, Mark, Matthew and Luke are grouped together as the Synoptic Gospels.

John, the last of the four Gospels, is significantly different, stimulating considerable debate about whether it should be included when the Bible was canonized. Written about 100 CE, it may represent a response to debates that were ongoing in the local churches of the time. It emphasizes Jesus' role as the Messiah and for the first time describes two opposing realms of good and evil in the world. One Bishop argued for its inclusion in the official canon because four was a desirable number. "Like the four zones of the world and the four directions of the wind...it is fitting that the church should have four pillars."

After he sanctioned Christianity as the official religion of the Roman Empire in 313, Constantine selected a church historian named Eusebius to produce fifty Bibles for his church in Constantinople. Eusebius selected texts from many Gospels that were circulating in different church communities of the time. In a long and contested process, Eusebius solidified the official canon. By 367, the Bishop of Alexandria was able to write (in an Easter letter) a list of the books of the New Testament that are recognized by most Catholic and Protestant churches today.

"Let man then learn the revelation of all nature and all thought to his heart; that the Highest dwells with him."

RALPH WALDO EMERSON

Philosophy: What can we learn from nature?

In the mid 1800's, a uniquely American literary, political and philosophical movement developed in New England which came to be called transcendentalism. It is an idealistic system of thought based on a belief in the basic goodness of humanity—a reaction to the sinful nature of man depicted by the dominant Christian churches of the day. It sees an essential unity of all creation, viewing the natural world as an expression of God, and it believes that the deepest truths are available through personal revelation. Two of my favorite writers, Ralph Waldo Emerson and Henry David Thoreau, were central figures in this movement.

Emerson was a critic of his contemporary society for its unthinking conformity. He urged individuals to find "an original relation to the universe." This included the search for a new understanding of religion, which was increasingly in conflict with emerging science. Biblical scholarship was casting doubts on long held beliefs about the Bible, while translations of scriptures from Eastern religions challenged traditional Western assumptions. In a harsh choice of words, Emerson concluded, *"The religions of the world are the ejaculations of a few imaginative men."* He believed that a real understanding of Truth could be achieved best by the use of the Divine gifts of intuition, insight and inspiration.

"A man should learn to detect and watch that gleam of light which flashes across his mind from within, more than the luster of the firmament of bards and sages."

"God enters by a private door into every individual."

"Our faith comes in moments, our vice is habitual. Yet there is depth in those brief moments which constrains us to ascribe more reality to them than to all other experiences."

"The whole course of things goes to teach us faith. We need only obey. There is guidance for each of us, and by lowly listening we shall hear the right word."

"Man is a stream whose source is hidden. Always our being is descending into us from we know not whence."

"...that Unity, that Over-soul, within which every man's particular being is contained and made one with all other; that common heart of which all sincere conversation is the worship, to which all right action is submission..."

"...there is no bar or wall in the soul, where man, the effect ceases, and God, the cause, begins."

"Love is omnipresent in nature as motive and reward. Love is our highest word and the synonym for God."

This theme of independent thought and action is carried over to non-religious areas in one of Emerson's most famous essays, *Self-reliance.*

"Whoso would be a man, must be a nonconformist."

"For non-conformity, the world whips you with its displeasure."

"No law can be sacred to me but that of my nature...the only right is what is after my constitution; the only wrong what is against it."

"I must be myself. I cannot break myself any longer for you, or you. If you love me for what I am we shall be happier. If you cannot, I will seek to deserve that you should. I must be myself. I will not hide my tastes or aversions. I will so trust that what is deep is holy, that I will do strongly before the sun and moon whatever inly rejoices me and the heart appoints."

Some of my other favorite wisdom from Emerson includes:

"Everything the individual sees without him corresponds to his states of mind..."

"Trust men and they will be true to you; treat them greatly and they will show themselves great."

"What you do speaks so loud, I cannot hear what you say."

Perhaps the best summary of Emerson's belief in the indwelling presence of God is expressed eloquently in this quote:

"From within or from behind, a light shines through us upon things and makes us aware that we are nothing, but the light is all. A man is the façade of a temple wherein all wisdom and good abide... When it breathes through his intellect, it is genius; when it breaths through his will, it is virtue; when it flows through his affection, it is love."

Even in pre-Civil War America, the transcendentalists were reacting to what they perceived to be an expanding commercialism and rampant materialism that they felt was damaging to the human spirit. Thoreau put his convictions into action on July 4, 1845 by declaring his "independence" and removing himself (at least by a mile and a half) from the bustling "city" of Concord. In a rustic cabin in the woods on the shore of Walden Pond (after which he named his most famous book), he practiced a life that followed his motto *Multum in parvo* – "much in little", or "simplicity".

"I went to the woods because I wished to live deliberately, to front only the essential facts of life, and see if I could learn what it had to teach, and not, when I come to die, discover that I had not lived."

"Our life is frittered away by details...In the midst of this chopping sea of civilized life, such are the clouds and storms and quicksands and thousand and one items to be allowed for...Simplify, simplify."

Thoreau would be disheartened by our technology driven, multitasking world. *"Our inventions are wont to be pretty toys, which distract our attention from serious things. They are but improved means to an unimproved end." "Men have become tools of their tools."*

Like Emerson, Thoreau saw God as existing not outside and separate from the world, but throughout the universe. He preferred, however, to develop his understanding of God through communion with nature rather than through introspection. Properly attuned to nature, one could perceive the Higher Laws that are expressions of Divine intention, which when understood, lead to true happiness.

"Blessed are those who never read a newspaper, for they shall see Nature and, through her, God." Of course, this view was in conflict with traditional church doctrine that set God above and apart from the world. *"The greater part of what my neighbors call good I believe in my soul to be evil, and if I repent of anything, it is very likely to be my good behavior."* Near the end of his life, a pious relative asked if Thoreau had made his peace with God and he famously replied, *"I am not aware that we ever quarreled."*

Thoreau was never one to worry about convention. One of his most well known quotes says, *"If a man does not keep pace with his companions, perhaps it is because he hears a different drummer. Let him step to the music that he hears, however measured or far away."*

Other favorite quotes from Thoreau include:

"I know of no more encouraging fact than the unquestioned ability of a man to elevate his life by conscious endeavor."

"Be true to your work, your word and your friend."

"That man is richest whose pleasures are the cheapest."

The words of Emerson and Thoreau have made me more aware of the lessons to be learned from the external world of nature and my internal world of introspection.

> **"In principle the great religions of the world do not differ as much as they appear to."**
>
> ERNEST HOLMES

Metaphysics: Can religion and philosophy be blended?

As I became aware of the variety of religions, philosophies and spiritual paths in the world, it seemed unlikely that one contained the truth and all the rest were false. I thought it was more likely that truth resided in some hybrid or "meta-understanding" of religion and philosophy. I later discovered a branch of philosophy called *metaphysics* that seeks this kind of understanding—of the relationship between humankind and the universe.

Aware that I was developing a concept of God that did not fit into any of the traditional boxes, I was reassured to learn that I was not the first. During the late 19th century, a spiritual movement began which came to be called *New Thought*. The three main branches of New Thought were Religious Science founded by Ernest Holmes, Unity founded by Charles and Myrtle Fillmore, and Church of Divine Science founded by Malinda Cramer. Although differing slightly in beliefs, they share fundamental principles that separate them from established religions.

New Thought was seeded from several areas of intellectual growth that were blossoming at the time. Advances in science, including Darwin's Theory of Evolution, were changing our understanding of humankind's place in the universe. Emerson's transcendentalism provided glimpses of a God that expressed throughout nature and was accessible through personal insight. Spiritual healing, as practiced by Phineas Quimby and Emma Curtis Hopkins, was interpreted as a natural extension of the teachings of Jesus. Sprinkled with a new awareness of Eastern philosophy and soaked with open-minded optimism, the New Thought movement began to germinate.

Ernest Holmes was a student of religion. He built his philosophy on the belief that there was a "Golden Thread of Truth" that runs through the fabric of all religions. In 1926, he published the culmination of his search in *The Science of Mind*. While still emphasizing the teachings of Jesus, his book interprets the Bible from a fresh metaphysical perspective based on the precepts of New Thought. Dr. Holmes stated, *"Religious Science is a correlation of laws of science, opinions of philosophy, and revelation of religion applied to human needs and the aspirations of man."*

In an attempt to describe and differentiate his idea of God from more traditional concepts, Holmes uses terms like "Infinite Intelligence", "Universal Mind," and "Creative Mind." For him, *"God is not ...a person, but a Universal Presence...already in our own soul, already operating through our own consciousness."*

In his credo called "What I believe," he clarifies:

We believe in God, the Living Spirit Almighty; one, indestructible, absolute and self-existent Cause. This One manifests itself in and through all creation, but is not absorbed by its creation. The manifest universe is the body of God; it is the logical and necessary outcome of the infinite self-knowingness of God.

We believe in the incarnation of the Spirit in all, and that we are all incarnations of the One Spirit.

We believe in the unity of all life, and that the highest God and the innermost God is one God.

We believe that God is personal to all who feel this indwelling Presence.

In such statements, Holmes is attempting to expand our understanding of God beyond anthropomorphic limits, a God who is more than Lawgiver and Ruler. Instead, he sees God as the One Source of an ongoing creation, an Infinite Intelligence present in all things, an Energy behind all activity in the cosmos.

Several key conclusions follow from such a definition of God. First, if God is all there is and God is good, then there is no room for a concept of an evil opposing force in the world. *"We believe in the eternal Goodness, the eternal Loving-kindness and the eternal Givingness of Life to all."* God is infinitely abundant, and all conceivable good is available to flow into human experience. Things we label as "bad" are the result of misguided desires and choices, or the random accidents necessary for us to have free will. "Evil" reflects a lack of perception of the big picture of life.

Second, a God that lives within us and expresses through us is always immediately accessible. *"We believe that the Kingdom of Heaven is within us and that we experience this Kingdom to the degree that we become conscious of it. We believe in the direct revelation of Truth through our intuitive and spiritual nature, and that anyone may become a revealer of Truth who lives in close contact with the Indwelling God."*

In this view, all people are seen as spiritual beings. The great spiritual teachers, such as Jesus and Buddha, are "way-showers"— manifestations of what humanity can become. They serve as examples of what is possible when we are attuned to the Divinity that dwells within each of us.

A cornerstone of New Thought is summarized in Dr. Holmes statement "Change your thinking, change your life." Not only do we express the Universal Mind within us, but in reciprocal fashion, our thoughts influence the Universal Mind. In other words, our thoughts effect the ongoing expression of the Creative Mind in the world. To paraphrase the words of Jesus, it is done to us as we believe.

As a result of this central tenant, prayer in New Thought is not about imploring an external power. Rather, it is about the holding of expectations in our mind that then create their own fulfillment.

"We believe that the Universal Spirit which is God, operates through a Universal Mind, which is the Law of God; and that we are surrounded by this Creative Mind which receives the direct impress of our thought and acts upon it. We believe in the healing of the sick through the power of this Mind. We believe in the control of conditions through the power of this Mind". Thus, mental states and attitudes manifest as our experience in daily living, and right thinking has a healing effect.

New Thought may sound like magical thinking—whatever one wishes for comes true. A shallow understanding can also cause anguish and guilt in people accused of bringing on their own illness by "bad thinking." A deeper understanding is more nuanced, and is increasingly supported by science.

We know, for example, that positive thoughts can influence our health, not by magic, but by changing stress hormones and cellular communication within our body. Also, the branch of physics called quantum mechanics provides evidence that our thoughts actually influence observable events in nature. (No, I can't explain it, but it is worth investigating for a deeper understanding.)

Modern knowledge of perception and brain function support the idea that we *do* create our own experience. Our interpretation of the events in our lives becomes our reality. To put it another way, *our life and our happiness is our choice.*

Developing faith in a Universal Presence that is expressed through us and throughout creation makes sense to me. It serves as the foundation of a positive approach to life. Such a metaphysical stance leads us to seek the good in all people and events. It also allows us to improve our quality of life by our choice of thoughts and attitudes. My personal experience has validated this approach for me.

"My religion consists of a humble admiration of the illimitable superior spirit who reveals himself in the slight details we are able to perceive with our frail and feeble mind." ALBERT EINSTEIN

God: Can I believe in both science and religion?

I have emphasized science in this writing. Understandable physical processes have shaped the universe and natural selection has shaped human beings. I have briefly outlined how political forces, social needs, and cognitive tendencies have shaped religions. Am I saying it is wise not to be religious? No, not at all. However, the popular conception of God that developed before modern science does need updating. Any credible religion must be compatible with our scientific knowledge.

At some point in our childhood development, we give up our notion of a Santa Claus that flies through the sky in a sled on Christmas Eve. I think, for the benefit of humanity, we need to give up the notion of the God of Michelangelo on the ceiling of the Sistine Chapel—muscular, gray haired, and stern faced. Our anthropomorphic concept of God has created problems, allowing Him to be seen as judgmental and punitive, responsive or unresponsive, jealous and vengeful. As a projection of simple humans, our God on the throne in the clouds takes sides and justifies war. We have even allowed Him to be a him.

Some have tried to use science to prove the existence of God. For example, they have calculated that an infinitesimal change of only $1/10^{59}$ in the explosive force of the big bang would have caused the universe to collapse back on itself or expand too rapidly for stars to form. Similar calculations have been done for the relationship between the forces of gravity and electromagnetism (required to produce the heavy elements necessary for life); the relationship between the nuclear weak force and gravity (necessary to produce water); and the precise strength of nuclear forces (required to make atoms).

This kind of evidence makes our "biofriendly" universe seem beyond chance and supports the idea of a Great Designer. Still, at least to this point, God remains outside scientific understanding.

I am not surprised that God is beyond our detection. Our sense organs evolved sensitivity to a small part of the information available in our physical environment. Our ears can only hear a portion of the vibrations that surround us, the portion we call sound. Our eyes detect a tiny fraction of the electromagnetic spectrum, the portion we call visible light. Naturally, our scientific instruments enhance the information of which we are already aware—it is hard to develop detectors for information that we do not even know exists.

When scientists start talking about dark matter and dark energy (which we cannot sense) and alternative universes (that may exist beyond our detection), it is clear how little of our universe (or universes) we actually perceive. In this context, it is not surprising that God remains beyond our physical senses and scientific instruments.

Then there is our poor, inadequate brain. I am willing to admit that I do not understand all of the physics concepts of relativity and quantum mechanics that brains such as Einstein's have come up with to explain the physical universe. How much more inadequate is my brain to comprehend the Incomprehensible or describe the Ineffable? Self-knowledge and honesty require me to accept that understanding the true nature of God is beyond my capability.

Does God simply surpass all human understanding? Is it reasonable to think that our brains, which evolved for survival and reproduction in this physical world, do not have the capacity for fully comprehending God?

That is what makes sense to me.

Many religions have a concept of God as unknowable and indescribable. For example, Jews acknowledge this ineffable nature of God by not spelling his name in writing. Yahweh becomes YHWH or God becomes G_d. As we have seen, Buddha refused to answer questions about the nature of God, seeing such discussions as hopelessly futile and distracting.

One thing we have observed is that religion is universal in nearly all cultures of the world as far back as we can see. To say that this is based solely on our need to explain the unexplainable, or represents an inevitable side effect of our socially enhanced brain, seems inadequate. I think it is more reasonable to conclude that the universality of religion is one of the strongest arguments *for* God. Like billions of people before me, my knowledge of God is not scientific, but personal. It is based on faith and experience.

Our best course may be to accept the Divine Mystery with humility and open ourselves to glimpses that penetrate the veil of our inadequacy. We must be careful of those who offer more clarity—especially when it is attached to intolerance and belligerent righteousness.

Many of us seem to yearn for a relationship with God. I do not think it is harmful to have a personal image of God that evokes a feeling state to which we can relate. It may be Jesus or Buddha, Mary or Divine Mother. It may be a mountain stream or the star-filled sky. What is essential is that we recognize that it is only a representation and we must attribute to it only the highest qualities that we are capable of imagining—loving compassion, nurturing acceptance, peaceful beauty.

So how can we respond to an infinite, omnipresent and mysterious God? If God is omnipresent, then every human being embodies the Divine. This provides clear guidance as I consider how I should treat my fellow human beings. If the Earth is an expression of God's creative presence, then it deserves my respect, appreciation and active care.

For some temperament types, Meditation (or Prayer) may provide the surest guideposts on the path to Enlightenment. As V. Raman has written, *"The most important realization of the Hindu seers, the fundamental revelation that comes from their meditation and spiritual search, is that beneath and beyond the material and physical world lies a spiritual reality. It's only when one recognizes this that one has truly lived a human life."*

Not everyone, however, is cut out to spend hours in meditative silence. The great spiritual teachers tell us there are many pathways to God. Some find Enlightenment through an intellectual search for Wisdom; some find it through unfailing Devotion; others may find it through selfless Service.

Eventually, you will find your own Path and develop a concept of God that works for you. *Those who find a personal connection to the Divine develop a deep inner knowing that is experienced as peace and expressed as love and compassion.*

I believe in God and I have faith in God. It is not a traditional concept of God, but one that has emerged from my lifelong exploration and is compatible with my knowledge of science. My limited understanding of God has been most aided by looking within. Prayer, meditation and introspection have provided more insights for me than books, sermons or dogma. I choose to believe that aspects of God's nature are expressed in human beings and that listening to the "still, small voice" inside me is the most inspired of sermons. I also believe that God is expressed in nature and that walking in awareness of that Beauty is like reading the holiest of scriptures.

An ancient Zen proverb says, "Before Enlightenment; chop wood, carry water. After Enlightenment; chop wood, carry water." (In our age of environmental consciousness, perhaps "grow trees, conserve water.") While you seek spiritual inspiration, *what is most important is how you live your life.*

V. Living with Wisdom

Dear Adam,

My generation grew up in the Cold War that began after World War II. It was a frightening time because the United States and the Soviet Union were in a nuclear arms race, with both countries expanding their arsenals of nuclear warheads and intercontinental ballistic missiles. The newspaper published diagrams showing concentric rings of destruction surrounding nearby Soviet nuclear missile target sites. The rings overlapped our home.

I watched television programs that showed disintegrating buildings and melting mannequins resulting from a nuclear blast. Then the programs would explain how to build a nuclear bomb shelter in your backyard to increase—slightly—your chances of survival.

I saw Nike air defense missiles in the hills above our home and we practiced "duck and cover" drills in our elementary school. The air raid sirens in our town blared every Friday, a test that reminded us of how close we were to annihilation. I knew that "duck and cover" was not going to keep me from being incinerated in a nuclear war.

Growing up in Southern California, many days were so smoggy I could not see across the school playground, and my lungs would burn if I tried to run. Pelicans were disappearing on the coast from the effects of the pesticide DDT, and beaches were covered with trash and oil tar. It was easy to feel that things were hopeless.

I tell you this to demonstrate that there is always hope. We did not all die in a nuclear holocaust and concerned citizens began an environmental movement that brought back the pelican and improved the air.

I imagine your generation faces challenges that may also seem insurmountable. Don't despair. Act instead— with a faith that good things happen when enough people make positive choices. Just as I believe that by the power of our choices we can lead a personally satisfying and fulfilling life, I also believe that together we have the power as human beings to create a healthy and peaceful world.

In this last section, I build on the previous chapters with some final thoughts on wisdom for your daily life.

With Love,
Grampy

Connect With Nature

Yosemite National Park is my favorite place in the world to hike and connect with nature. Not surprisingly, I love the writings of John Muir (1838-1914), the patron saint of the environmental movement. His devoted activism inspired the National Park System and saved Yosemite from development. He had a gift for poetically expressing the sensations and feelings one may experience while walking in awareness of the natural world. I have selected a few John Muir quotes that are definitely part of my favorite wisdom. If you enjoy this sample, I highly recommend a deeper exploration of the writings of this amazing man.

"Walk away quietly in any direction and taste the freedom of the mountaineer. Camp out among the grasses and gentians of glacial meadows, in craggy garden nooks full of nature's darlings. Climb the mountains and get their good tidings, Nature's peace will flow into you as sunshine flows into trees. The winds will blow their own freshness into you and the storms their energy, while cares will drop off like autumn leaves. As age comes on, one source of enjoyment after another is closed, but nature's sources never fail."

"Come to the woods, for here is rest. There is no repose like that of the green deep woods. Here grow the wallflower and the violet. The squirrel will come and sit upon your knee, the logcock will wake you in the morning. Sleep in forgetfulness of all ill. Of all the upness accessible to mortals, there is no upness comparable to the mountains."

"Looking eastward from the summit of Pacheco Pass one shining morning, a landscape was displayed that after all my wanderings still appears as the most beautiful I have ever beheld. At my feet lay the Great Central Valley of California, level and flowery, like a lake of pure sunshine, forty or fifty miles wide, five hundred miles long, one rich furred garden of yellow Compositae. And from the eastern boundary of this vast golden flower-bed rose the mighty Sierra, miles in height, and so gloriously colored and so radiant, it seemed not clothed with light but wholly composed of it, like the wall of some celestial city.... Then it seemed to me that the Sierra should be called, not the Nevada or Snowy Range, but the Range of Light. And after ten years of wandering and wondering in the heart of it, rejoicing in its glorious floods of light, the white beams of the morning streaming through the passes, the noonday radiance on the crystal rocks, the flush of the alpenglow, and the irised spray of countless waterfalls, it still seems above all others the Range of Light."

"All the wild world is beautiful, and it matters but little where we go, to highlands or lowlands, woods or plains, on the sea or land or down among the crystals of waves or high in a balloon in the sky; through all the climates, hot or cold, storms and calms, everywhere and always we are in God's eternal beauty and love. So universally true is this, the spot where we chance to be always seems the best."

"Oh, these vast, calm, measureless mountain days, inciting at once to work and rest! Days in whose light everything seems equally divine, opening a thousand windows to show us God. Nevermore, however weary, should one faint by the way who gains the blessings of one mountain day; whatever his fate, long life, short life, stormy or calm, he is rich forever."

"I used to envy the father of our race, dwelling as he did in contact with the new-made fields and plants of Eden; but I do so no more, because I have discovered that I also live in "creation's dawn." The morning stars still sing together, and the world, not yet half made, becomes more beautiful every day."

"No synonym for God is so perfect as Beauty. Whether as seen carving the lines of the mountains with glaciers, or gathering matter into stars, or planning the movements of water, or gardening—still all is Beauty!"

"There is a love of wild nature in everybody, an ancient mother-love ever showing itself whether recognized or no, and however covered by cares and duties."

"Brought into right relationships with the wilderness, man would see that his appropriation of Earth's resources beyond his personal needs would only bring imbalance and begat ultimate loss and poverty by all."

"A few minutes ago every tree was excited, bowing to the roaring storm, waving, swirling, tossing their branches in glorious enthusiasm like worship. But though to the outer ear these trees are now silent, their songs never cease."

"Few are altogether deaf to the preaching of pine trees. Their sermons on the mountains go to our hearts; and if people in general could be got into the woods, even for once, to hear the trees speak for themselves, all difficulties in the way of forest preservation would vanish.

"Keep close to Nature's heart... and break clear away, once in awhile, and climb a mountain or spend a week in the woods. Wash your spirit clean."

"I only went out for a walk, and finally concluded to stay out till sundown, for going out, I found, was really going in."

John Muir

"Man did not weave the web of life—he is merely a strand in it. Whatever he does to the web, he does to himself."

Stand Against Ecocide

As I have mentioned, one of the reasons that humans are so genetically similar is that we descended from a relatively small population of ancestors, perhaps as few as 2,000 – 20,000 individuals. Before the agricultural revolution (10,000 BCE), world human population was still probably under one million. The following graph shows the exponential growth of the human population after the industrial revolution.

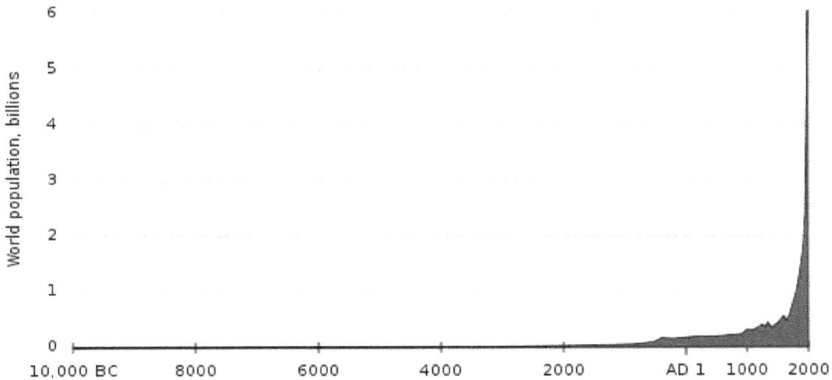

From the perspective of the global ecology of life on earth, humans have been a disaster. To provide for the needs of our increasing population—who desire an increasing standard of living—we are rapidly depleting worldwide resources. Simultaneously, the waste products from our consumption are poisoning the planet.

Nature has given us powerful instincts for reproduction that were necessary for the survival of our species early in its evolution. Now it is imperative for us to use our awareness and intelligence to bring human population under control. As a rule, education and a higher standard of living have reduced birth rates in industrialized societies. We must all act in ways that support a responsible worldwide culture—one that recognizes the connection between overpopulation, environmental degradation, and reduced quality of life for the people of all countries.

Of particular concern is the effect, often irreparable, of human populations on other forms of life on earth. This has a long historical precedent. Within 5,000 years after humans arrived in Australia, nearly ninety percent of large marsupial species had become extinct. Within a few thousand years after human migration into the New World, 135 species of mammals were wiped out, including three-fourths of the larger species. In recent times, the 40 million bison that roamed the Great Plains of North America in 1800 were hunted to near extinction in less than 100 years. The same story has been told repeatedly around the world.

We might pardon the actions of our ancestors who were struggling for survival (or acted in ignorance). But we no longer have excuses for treating other forms of life with such callous disregard.

In 2009, an estimated 8,000 animal species and 9,000 plant species were at risk of extinction. This endangered list includes 1/3 of all amphibians, nearly 1/2 of all turtles and tortoises, 1/5 of all mammals and 1/8 of all birds.

Aquatic environments are also affected. Nearly all of the earth's coral reefs have been damaged by human activities and half may be destroyed in the next few decades. Our once boundless supply of commercial fish has been depleted by overfishing. No natural habitat has escaped our debasement.

The overall pace of extinction on the planet is estimated to be anywhere from 100 to 1,000 times the normal historic rate. World-renowned biologist E. O. Wilson has warned that half of all species of life may become extinct by the end of this century.

An estimated eighty percent of species loss today is caused by habitat destruction. The greatest damage to natural habitats has been the result of our expanding need for agricultural land to feed our growing population. This is one factor behind the loss of 160,000 square kilometers of tropical rainforest annually. Containing our richest treasures of biodiversity, we have destroyed nearly half of the original tropical rainforests in the world.

We also cover over huge areas of land with highways, parking lots and buildings during urbanization. This sprawl of development is occurring at five times the rate of population growth. One aspect of this development has been the loss of more than 50% of the wetlands in the United States since our founding.

Another factor that will increase the rate of extinction is global warming. Scientific consensus is strong that carbon dioxide waste from burning fossil fuels is responsible for our dramatic climate change. Many species may not survive in the changing ecosystems that higher average temperatures produce.

I hope that by the time you read this, these trends have been reversed. Given our increasing population size and demand for resources, I am not optimistic about the immediate future.

In the long term, I would like to believe that education will provide the motivation and new technologies will provide the means for us to live in greater harmony with the natural world. I agree with the sentiment expressed by G. H. Brundtland, former Prime Minister of Norway, who said, *"We must consider our planet to be on loan from our children, rather than being a gift from our ancestors."*

May you and your children still have access to the peace, beauty, and inspiration found in nature.

At this point, I pause to add a personal story:

When your father was young and we went camping as a family, we always performed a ritual. After we had rolled up our tents and packed up our gear, we would take a few minutes to walk our campsite and pick up any trash that we could find. Most of it was not ours, but I told your father that it was our responsibility to leave the campsite cleaner than we found it. I explained that if everybody did the same, we would always have clean and beautiful campsites to go to in the future.

Of course, this may seem like a small thing, a barely noticeable contribution to environmental stewardship. In addition, we knew that the campers that came after us might not act as responsibly, but this did not matter. What mattered was that we acted with integrity—consistent with our beliefs and values.

Even when you are in the minority, your choices influence those around you. When enough people decide to make the effort to act responsibly, there is a shift in the culture—a change in the group consciousness. We have seen it before in such areas as buckling up young children in car seats, not smoking in confined public spaces, recycling bottles and cans, and picking up after our dogs.

Government laws and regulations will help, but they must be supported by the responsible choices of individuals. The end of ecocide will only come when enough people recognize the value of our natural world and do the things necessary to preserve it.

Our small, everyday choices make a life honoring statement.

I hope that you will consider this a family legacy. Make the choices that support life in all its forms. If you have your own children, pass along an attitude of appreciation and respect when you take them to visit the natural places that remain in our world.

**"World peace must develop from inner peace.
Peace is not just the absence of violence, but
the manifestation of human compassion."**

DALAI LAMA

Be The Peace

In October of 1990, fifteen year old Nayirah testified before the
Congressional Human Rights Caucus. She claimed to be a Kuwaiti
refugee who was a volunteer nurse in a maternity ward of a
hospital in Kuwait City. She described in vivid detail how she had
witnessed the murder of infant children by invading Iraqi soldiers.
"They took the babies out of the incubator, took the incubators,
and left the babies to die on the cold floor," she testified. Her
testimony came at a critical time when the Bush administration
was trying to galvanize support for military action to eject the Iraq
army from Kuwait.

After her testimony, the United States Senate voted 52-47 in
support of the Gulf War of 1991. Seven Senators publicly sited
Nayirah's report as being influential in their vote—a decision that
would have gone the other way with a change in only three votes.

It was later disclosed that "Nurse Nayirah" was actually the
daughter of the Kuwaiti ambassador to the US. A public relations
firm, hired by the Kuwaiti government to gain support for the
Kuwaiti cause, had arranged her testimony before the Senate
Committee. Doctors at the hospital reported that the Iraqis
removed no incubators, and no babies had been removed from
them. After the war had begun, Nayirah admitted that she was
never a volunteer at the hospital, had "only stopped by for a few
minutes" and had seen one baby outside of an incubator "for no
more than a moment." But the damage was already done.

The second President Bush used unsubstantiated intelligence about weapons of mass destruction to gain support for the Iraq war of 2003. The Johnson administration exaggerated reports from a Gulf of Tonkin "incident" to escalate the War in Vietnam in 1964. If you look closely at history, it seems that a few powerful men often generate war by manipulating their populations into combat.

Average citizens generally desire to live out their lives in peace. Tragically, those that rise to leadership, for a variety of personal and political reasons, sometimes march their countries down the road to war. They take advantage of our innate tendency to retaliate against those identified as outside aggressors.

In a perfect world, there would be no war, but imperfect humans sometimes rise to power. Most would agree that real aggressors must be constrained and tyrants who commit atrocities must be stopped. However, citizens have a moral duty to keep a check on the aspirations of those in power and not be misled into unjustified wars.

One strategy used by those in power to make war more palatable is to characterize the enemy as less than human. This has been documented in tribal societies where only those within the tribe are called by the name for "people" or "human." This makes the killing of members of other tribes morally acceptable. Members of my generation sent to fight the Vietnam War were taught derogatory slang terms for the Vietnamese in boot camp. After being trained to hate the North Vietnamese as subhuman savages, it was easier to rain violence on them.

Humans are not the only species with organized violence, but we are unique in our capacity to abstract our aggression over time and space. We can be violently aggressive against unknown individuals and groups, inventing and utilizing technology to make our violence more efficient.

Some early psychological studies seemed to suggest that racism and xenophobia (fear and hatred of foreigners) were "hard wired" in our brains. Subjects shown photos of faces from different races or cultures than their own (even subliminally—below conscious awareness) had activated amygdala responses of fear and anxiety.

Later studies determined that those fear responses were dependent on many subtle variables, including context and preexisting racism. For example, faces of celebrities from different races did not trigger a fear response, presumably because of familiarity. Also, if clues were first given that allowed the subject to think about the image as an individual, the xenophobic fear response was not triggered. The conclusion is that racism has a learned component and fear of those that are different is not automatic.

Even in my lifetime, tremendous progress has been made against racism, stereotyping, and prejudice. Although much remains to be done, I am hopeful that the social integration of societies, worldwide communication capabilities, and increased mixing of populations will eventually make this topic obsolete. That should make it more difficult for leaders to use xenophobic fears as a pretext for war. (Although differences in religion or culture still seem to generate fear and hatred in some.)

With the blessings of freedom come responsibilities. Even if politics and government are not a natural interest for you, you have the duty in a democracy to be informed and actively participate in your own governance. This is even more vital in an age where sophistication in mass media and the psychology of manipulation require vigilant analysis of political messages. For the benefit of your family, your community, your country, and humanity, I hope that you will be an informed and active citizen.

Not only do we have a responsibility to create the government we want, we have a responsibility to create the society we want. If we accept beliefs of victimization and justified revenge, we support a culture of violence. If we contribute to an authoritarian culture that is conforming, rigid and unreflective, we support a culture of violence. If we do not provide all children with a safe and nurturing environment in which to learn and grow, we perpetuate a culture of violence.

Individuals who stand for nonviolence, who are open to new understanding, and who provide love and support for the next generation can transform society.

We may never have a society that is entirely free of violence. Aggressiveness and the capacity for violence are part of our biological history. Yet we know that some societies are much less violent than others, and that the precursors to violence in our society can be reduced with conscious effort.

Peace begins at a personal level—as an absence of violence in the way we conduct our daily life. A common slogan among antiwar activists is "Teach Peace." However, as is usually the case, we teach more by our actions than we do by our words. A less violent world begins with the cultivation of attitudes that model peace as a way of life, including the way we speak to one another.

Many have commented on an increase in the coarseness and rudeness of society in recent decades. If the culture is to be turned in a more civil direction, it will be because individuals refuse to compromise their personal values—and lead by example. Remember that both positive and negative transformative memes can spread quickly through a connected culture. Express peace in word and action.

"Let there be peace on earth, and let it begin with me."
Jill Jackson Miller

> **"Men are not prisoners of fate, but only prisoners of their own minds."**
>
> FRANKLIN D. ROOSEVELT

Manage Your Multimind

The world has changed more than our minds. As Robert Ornstein has written in his book *Multimind*, *"We are animals with a brain and mental system primarily organized around a few basic necessities: keeping warm and safe, minding the body and organizing our actions around the short-term contingencies of our environment. It is the system that 'got us here'."*

We have learned that a large portion of that mental system evolved to manage our social connections. Understanding our multimind—the neural networks that compete for our attention and control of our behavior—may help us to make better choices and live happier lives.

As discussed in the essay called *Mind*, our multimind is in many ways a simple mind. We pay attention to small portions of our available input. We focus on the most immediate and dramatic of events. We simplify our complex world to a level that is manageable—but highly inaccurate. Because of our multiple mind modules, we sometimes do not know why we behave as we do and we must rationalize our own actions to maintain our sense of mental integrity. The imperfect functioning of our limited minds has serious consequences.

When Marilyn Monroe committed suicide, the overall suicide rate in the USA increased by 12 percent and remained elevated for months. In 1999, after two students at Columbine High School in Colorado killed thirteen of their fellow students, the incidence of violent threats increased on campuses across the country. In Pennsylvania alone, there were 350 threats of school violence in the fifty days following the massacre, compared to a normal rate of two per year.

We could speculate about the activation of mirror neurons or the temporary alteration of cultural memes, but for whatever the reason, negative patterns can spread through a culture.

When Oprah Winfrey promoted the concept of "random acts of kindness" on her popular television show, the level of such activity spiked around the country. Positive thoughts and actions can also spread ("go viral") through our culture just like negative ones. Clearly, we can use the tendency of our simple mind to imitate and "follow the crowd" to improve our society. Choose carefully what you pass along to others.

Awareness of our simple-minded nature is an excellent first step toward higher functioning. One aspect of our mind that can have consequences ranging from smoking to genocide is our tendency toward conformity. Although it is difficult to admit, we have a strong desire to feel connected to and accepted by others—sometimes at the expense of our own integrity.

In a classic experiment by Solomon Asch, subjects were shown a line and then asked to select a matching line from several choices of different lengths. When a group of six confederates (all in on the experiment) picked an obviously wrong answer, 32% of subjects conformed to the unspoken group pressure by also selecting the wrong answer. If even one confederate picked the correct answer (different from the rest of the confederates), the subject's conformity dropped to only 8%.

In a related experiment, 85% of subjects tried to help a student that they thought was having an epileptic seizure in the next room. If they were part of a group when they heard the distress next door, only 30% tried to help, apparently believing that since no one else was responding it must be alright to do nothing.

I hope you will stand tall for what you believe in, even when you are walking against the winds of conformity.

Our desire to "fit in" is only one aspect of our mind used by corporations and politicians to manipulate our thinking. Be conscious that neuromarketers and political neurostrategists are using the weaknesses of your simple mind to attempt to manipulate your decision-making. This is vital for saving your money and your democracy.

We know, for example, that most people's minds seek easy answers and congruent beliefs. If a media conglomerate wanted to disguise politically slanted news coverage, they might choose a corporate motto like "fair and balanced." Our minds do not want to deal with the incongruence of words and actions, so we accept the slogan as if it were a statement of fact.

Pundits, blogs and websites often distort ("spin") information while implying that they are dispensing the impartial truth behind current events. Many people now seem to read or listen only to media that supports their existing belief systems, resulting in an increasingly polarized, intolerant and misinformed society. Listening critically to arguments on both sides of an issue will help you make a better judgment.

If a food company wanted to imply that their highly sugared cereal was nutritious, it might place a large banner on the box with words like "all natural" or "heart healthy." If a drug company wanted to sell more pills, it might advertise them as safe and effective based on "clinical trials." Advertisers know that very few minds will have the skills (or want to expend the energy) to challenge the scientific validity of their claims.

Whether buying cereal or "buying" a politician, avoid being manipulated. Pay attention to attempts to tap into your subconscious motivations, particularly your desires for relationship, sex and belonging. It is wise to remain aware of techniques that others may use to influence you. Such vigilance will help keep your decisions informed and independent.

As previously discussed, another weakness of our simple mind is our tendency to focus on the immediate and the sensational. For example, in the last couple of years, three natural disasters have grabbed the headlines: a powerful hurricane flooded New Orleans; a massive Tsunami overwhelmed coastal Indonesia; and a devastating earthquake destroyed much of Haiti. In each case—at least for a few weeks—there was a massive outpouring of international aid and charitable giving for the victims. Yet during the same period of time, famine and epidemic disease took many more lives around the world without ever generating a headline. Our simple minds are drawn to the dramatic—and ignore the background noise of ongoing tragedy.

This is not meant as an indictment of human callousness. It merely stands as a testament to the natural tendencies of our "call me when something new happens" mind.

Sometimes our "wheeling and dealing" mind modules can take us on a wild ride. Reaching our long-term goals may require us to work toward more personal consistency and integration through self-control. This is no easy task. It may at times seem like a diplomatic mission, full of appeasement and compromise with our conflicting mind modules.

Be a loving parent to your mind, encouraging some independence and risk-taking without compromising safety. Allow for give and take between modules when necessary, but "set limits" when it is in your long-term best interest. Managing our multimind is a lot like house-training a puppy. Accidents are bound to happen. Consistency and perseverance eventually pay off.

Of course, there is always wisdom in not taking things too seriously. Sometimes our only salvation is the ability to laugh at ourselves, accepting our multimind as part of human nature.

"You can fool all the people some of the time, and some of the people all the time, but you cannot fool all the people all the time."

ABRAHAM LINCOLN

"It is wise to remember that you are one of those who can be fooled some of the time."

LAURENCE J. PETER

Don't Be Fooled

I love magic. I enjoy trying to figure out how I have been fooled and I appreciate the skill involved in a well-performed illusion. Unfortunately, some people confuse clever entertainment with reality, and this can be dangerous.

I once heard a psychologist tell a story about becoming a palm reader to generate part-time income while he was in college. He did not believe in palm reading, but in order to be credible, he read some books and tried to interpret the lines in the traditional way. To his astonishment, his clients consistently raved about his accuracy and seemed convinced of his psychic power.

To satisfy his own curiosity, he decided to try reading the lines exactly opposite of the way he had learned in the books. His clients continued to rave about his accuracy. It turned out that it did not matter how he "read" the palms, the only thing that mattered was that he present himself in a convincing way. Once the clients saw him as credible, they used the power of their own imagination to make the reading fit the circumstances of their own life. The same principle applies to psychic readings, communicating with the dead, fortune telling, astrology and any number of related activities that imply super-normal powers.

This ability of our creative mind to find connections and patterns in seemingly random events is the basis of superstition. At some level, we want to believe that our world is predictable. Take a statement I have often heard, "Bad things come in threes." When an event like a natural disaster or death of a famous person occurs, our mind can easily find two other incidents that occurred in the same period. After all, our mind can choose which events qualify and adjust the time period to fit the required criteria.

When a "psychic" tells us that "an unexpected monetary windfall is coming your way," our creative mind will search for events that fit the pattern, whether it is finding a coin on the sidewalk or a dollar in our coat pocket.

One technique designed to take advantage of our creative mind is called a *Barnum statement*, named after the famed American showman P.T. Barnum. It consists of a generality which may sound very personal, but which in fact applies to most people. "You are having problems with a friend or relative." "You are sometimes insecure, but hide it well." A related technique is called the *rainbow ruse*, which covers all the bases: "Some people think of you as quiet and shy, but when the mood strikes, you can become the center of attention." *Shot gunning* provides the client with a laundry list of possibilities from which to choose. "I see a heart problem in an important male in the family—a father, a grandfather, an uncle, a cousin." Your creative mind will find someone who fits. After all, we want the psychic to succeed!

In a scientific test of astrology, one group received personal horoscopes written by a professional astrologer and a second group receives the *same* horoscopes randomly assigned. Both groups gave the horoscopes equally high ratings for accuracy!

When we read an online horoscope for fun, that is entertainment. When a President uses an astrologer to inform foreign policy (rumored about Ronald Reagan), that is foolish.

Just because you cannot immediately figure out how you are being tricked does not mean something must be real. In today's world of digitally altered photos and computer generated images, the old saying "seeing is believing" no longer applies. Remaining cautious and skeptical is a prudent stance in a world where some are highly skilled at fooling us.

In the retail world, one common technique for fooling us is called *bait and switch*. This is where a product or service is advertised for a low price, but a salesperson then says it is "sold out" or uses some other ruse to get you to buy a more expensive item. A close relative to bait and switch is called *upselling*—a technique taught by most retailers from restaurants to technology stores. In this case, additional items are offered after the original product is ordered ("Do you want fries with that?" "Would you like to extend that warranty?") Being aware of these techniques can help you guard against wasting your money.

So, in this wisdom essay am I concerned with you being fooled by a palm reader or eating too many French-fries?   No. Sometimes being fooled can be important.

Matthew 7:15 "Beware of false prophets, who come to you in sheep's clothing but inwardly are ravenous wolves. 16You will know them by their fruits."

Jesus is speaking here of false religious leaders, but the same caution applies to many who want to mislead us. "False prophets" can be anybody from investment advisors to biased newscasters, from politicians to advertisers. Keep a skeptics eye on anyone who wants your vote, your money or your loyalty.

An area where being fooled can be particularly dangerous is in the selection of health care products and practices. The selling of herbs, vitamins, diets and exercise routines has become a multibillion-dollar industry.

Everybody wants to be healthy and youthful and many people hope to achieve these goals with quick solutions. Infomercials and online ads bombard us with easy ways to improve our appearance, weight, energy, sex lives and longevity. These shortcuts can waste our money—or worse, damage our health.

One technique to watch out for is the use of "scientific proof" for the effectiveness of a product or program. Science is easily manipulated when the scientist has an agenda. A researcher may influence experimental results in many ways, including taking advantage of *the placebo effect*. As you may know, the use of inactive ingredients for treatment can be 30-80% as effective as real medications. For example, saline (salt-water) injections for postoperative pain are as effective as a 6-8mg dose of morphine, and sugar pills are 75% as effective as antidepressant medication.

This phenomenon has been shown to be more that just fooling our brain. It exemplifies the close connection between mind and body. Expectation produces measurable changes in brain chemistry, which effect both perception and body function.

My point here is that scientists can manipulate research to "prove" the value of medications, supplements and treatments. Again, we are easily fooled when we want to believe.

Making good healthcare and lifestyle decisions is challenging enough without the forces that seek to mislead us. Be suspect of information provided by anyone who stands to profit from the sale of products or services. Look for evidence that is objective.

Enjoy the show.

"Clarity of mind means clarity of passion, too; this is why a great and clear mind loves ardently and sees distinctly what it loves."

BLAISE PASCAL (1623 - 1662)

Follow Your Heart

Following your heart means living with passion and expressing your true nature. As you grow and mature, you will develop interests that bring deep satisfaction. You will also develop ways of expressing your unique talents. Pursuing your interests and using your talents leads to personal fulfillment.

A wise minister once told me that the secret to happiness is to find your gifts and then give them away. He then clarified the importance of the double meaning in his statement as follows:

"Give them away" obviously means using your talents to be of service to others. Numerous studies have shown that helping others is one of the surest ways to find happiness and satisfaction. This is a fundamental *Wisdom Principle* of living (as discussed later).

Cleverly, "give them *a way*" can also mean finding the pathway that allows you to *use* your gifts. It is ideal if your vocation is an extension of your passions, because then it is not work. If you have not yet found a career that expresses your talents and fires your passion, however, it becomes even more beneficial to develop ways of using your gifts outside of your job.

Another fundamental source of our happiness is relationship. Nothing in life is more important than love and friendship.

How do we find true friends? One key is to be yourself—to express your true nature. Those who will make genuine friends will automatically be attracted to you. Even though most of us are skilled at presenting a facade that we think others will like, deep down we want to be accepted and appreciated for ourselves.

If you are a teenager now, the prospect of being yourself in front of others can be uncomfortable. As your self-confidence grows, you will realize that you cannot please everyone without compromising your integrity. If you live in Principle—treating others with respect and kindness while remaining true to yourself—your connections with others will come honestly and naturally, and the friendships you make will be real.

The best way to make a true friend is to be a true friend. This means listening, respecting privacy, appreciating differences and sharing common interests and activities.

Also, keep in mind that every relationship ends. Accepting this truth helps deepen our appreciation of relationships and reduces our suffering when life brings change.

As Ann Morrow Lindbergh wrote, *"We have so little faith in the ebb and flow of life, of love, of relationships. We leap at the flow of the tide and resist in terror its ebb. We are afraid it will never return. We insist on permanency, on duration, on continuity; when the only continuity possible, in life as in love, is in growth, in fluidity, in freedom, in the sense that dancers are free, barely touching as they pass, but partners in the same pattern."*

I love this description of relationship. It is natural for friendships to wax and wane as our interests evolve and we grow as individuals. A lifelong friend is a rare jewel to be cherished, but every relationship should be honored as a contribution to life's treasure. Each relationship has something to teach us.

Two types of relationship express deeper bonds than friendship. One is the committed love between devoted life partners and the other is the love between parent and child. These relationships are the peak of human experience because they rise out of our evolutionary core. Love is the most powerful expression of our humanity. It can also be the clearest window to spiritual light.

Feeling attraction to another is an experience to savor with delight. It is a programmed response to a variety of physical and psychological stimuli, yet it brings out the highest expressions of our human nature—in poetry, art and music. Such attraction, combined with a rapid breakdown of barriers, we call falling in love.

If things progress, falling in love becomes being in love, a physiological condition based on changes in brain chemistry. Current research is just beginning to explore the chemicals and brain areas involved. (I am a romantic at heart, so I hope references to hormones and neurotransmitters will not detract from an appreciation of love.) The heart-racing excitement and blinding euphoria of being in love can be as addicting as a drug.

Yet, while one of life's peak experiences, being in love is not the sole prerequisite to a healthy and lasting relationship. This confusion is at the root of the disheartening divorce statistics in the United States. The physiological high of being in love is temporary, eventually replaced by deeper levels of love in successful long-term relationships. *Mature love is not a condition, but an action.*

Central to any successful marriage or long-term relationship is friendship. When the brain chemicals of sexual attraction and being in love fade (as they inevitably do), you want a life partner who is your best friend. Such a friendship flows from a deep respect and appreciation for the other person. Only from these feelings can a mature love grow to replace the temporary condition of being in love.

As you evaluate a potential long-term relationship, some things to look for are shared interests, values and goals. Shared activities act like relationship glue. While each person may have separate interests or work in different fields, some mutual interests support the friendship that is at the heart of any healthy relationship.

As Antoine de Saint-Exupery said, "Love does not consist in gazing at each other, but in looking outward together in the same direction."

Whatever spiritual principles you adopt to guide you, it is helpful if your life partner shares them. Maintaining and practicing your values is hard in a culture with so many diverse beliefs. Having the support of someone who shares your values helps you build the faith that comes from living in Principle. Sharing spiritual growth as a couple is deeply bonding.

As with friendship, the best way to keep a committed relationship healthy is to *be the partner that you would like to have* and to *give more to the relationship than you receive.* This may sound obvious, but it requires a conscious effort. With all of the distractions that absorb our time, it is easy to neglect our relationship and take our partner for granted. Relationships require nurturing maintenance. My favorite definition of love comes from Eric Fromm: "Love is the active concern for the life and growth of that which we love."

I have been very blessed in love. I wish the same for you.

How do you find someone to love? In my experience, love finds you—when you are not looking for it. The quotes below explain this idea, another of life's great paradoxes:

> *"Those that go searching for love only make manifest their own lovelessness, and the loveless never find love, only the loving find love, and they never have to seek it."*
>
> D. H. Lawrence

> *"Love and you shall be loved."*
>
> Ralph Waldo Emerson

> *"If you want to be loved, love and be lovable."*
>
> Benjamin Franklin

"In the attitude of silence the soul finds the path in a clearer light, and what is elusive and deceptive resolved itself into crystal clearness."

MAHATMA GANDHI

Seek In Silence

One thing I notice when I visit with young people today is their abhorrence of silence. The television is on (even if not watched) or music is blaring day and night. A mobile internet connection or a headset plugged in to entertainment is necessary for leaving the house. If this describes your lifestyle, I offer the following for consideration.

Many years ago, I read a book titled *Four Arguments for the Elimination of Television.* (It might be updated today to *Four Arguments for the Elimination of Social Media.*) It made a very powerful case against television as a time-sink that damaged our mental health, physical health, relationships and society.

I lived without a television for many months at one point in my life (for economic, not philosophical reasons). Even though I do watch television today, I must admit that life without TV had many benefits. I luxuriated in the silence and found time for reading, writing and other pastimes that were highly satisfying. Appreciating these experiences, I try to maintain a balance of activities that include quiet time without background noise. It may feel uncomfortable at first, but I suggest you try the experiment.

A second observation of the younger generation is the proliferation of multitasking as a way of life. Many young people today report feeling bored if they are not watching media, instant messaging, exploring the web and listening to music—all at the same time. Sometimes they manage to squeeze school study or job tasks in the middle. Gaming, messaging, browsing, watching—the day is a whirlwind of activity and stimulation. This life pace can be exciting, but mind modules run amok can be a form of addiction.

Is there anything wrong with living life with hyper-stimulation? Scientists are just beginning to investigate this question, but evidence already indicates that multitasking detracts from task performance, even though multitaskers will swear that they can "do it all" without detriment.

Diminished task performance is only one price that may be paid by the constant multitasker. Many psychologists and spiritual teachers talk about the benefits of *mindfulness*—that is, giving your full attention to the here and now. Dr. Daniel Siegel of UCLA has gathered evidence that practicing mindfulness enhances physical health (by reducing stress), fosters emotional balance and deepens self-understanding.

I was once in a mindfulness workshop where the instructor asked us to place one raisin in our mouth without chewing or swallowing it. We were to focus all of our attention on the aroma, taste, texture and other qualities of our interaction with the raisin. It became a sensual experience. The lesson: we often miss out on the richness of life because we hurry and don't pay attention. You may not need an extended interaction with a raisin, but sometimes a meal can be a fuller sensory experience if you practice mindfulness.

It is like the difference between eating a packaged donut and a delicate French pastry. Both can satisfy hunger. Both may stimulate the sweet pleasure centers. But a finely prepared pastry offers experiences in textures, flavors and aromas that are not found in a packaged donut. Yet you will never know the difference if you don't put down the package of donuts (of superficial experience) and seek out pastries (of mindfulness) which offer a richer, more nuanced, more expansive satisfaction.

There is a difference between activity and achievement, between satiation and satisfaction, between fun and fulfillment. Don't settle for packaged donut experiences. Savor life with mindfulness.

Mindfulness also helps deepen our relationships. Just as mindfulness of the senses can enrich your awareness and appreciation, so mindfulness of other people can enrich your interactions and enhance connections. Take the time to really *be* with the people who count in your life.

> *"The most precious gift we can offer others is our presence. When mindfulness embraces those we love, they will bloom like flowers."*   Thich Nhat Hanh

Technology and the search for *quantity* in relationship have reduced the *quality* of our communication. Non-verbal cues from body language and voice tone are missing in communications that are common today. In texting, twittering and social networking, brevity and superficiality seem to be the dominant virtues.

I know my temperament type likes deep and meaningful relationships. Even though this preference is not universal, I can't help but think that many are left a little poorer by today's communication memes. A text or tweet may stimulate our social pleasure centers (communication as grooming), but it rarely contains the self-revelation that brings two people closer together. Social media (do you still have "Facebook?") tend to develop performance skills rather than intimacy skills.

Also, take the time to *be* with yourself. Have you ever had the experience of being alone and relaxed such as in the shower or on a walk, when you get an important idea that seems to come out of nowhere? In my experience, there is a deep level of mind, perhaps a "metamodule," that provides insights, sparks creativity and solves problems. It is only available to me when I am feeling safe, not interacting with others, and disengaged from tasks that require my full focus. Giving yourself the gift of some quiet alone time each day is not an inefficiency, but instead may be some of the most valuable and productive time that you can have. Some people formalize this alone time and call it meditation.

Dr. Herbert Benson wrote a book titled *The Relaxation Response* in which he details the physiological benefits associated with meditation and separates them from any religious interpretation. Benson and others have shown that following certain steps leads to stimulation of the parasympathetic nervous system—the body's antidote to the stress response of fight or flight. The benefits include lowered blood pressure, improved digestion, better immune function, increased energy, uplifted mood and reduction of damaging stress hormones. As little as ten to fifteen minutes set aside a couple of times a day can provide a noticeable impact on mind and body.

Here is an outline of some simple steps that can stimulate the relaxation response. Find a safe and quiet environment, assume a comfortable seated posture (floor or chair), and relax the body one area at a time. Gently lift closed eyes and focus attention on slow, deep breaths. With each breath, mentally repeat a word or phrase of personal choice such as "peace" or "love surrounds me." Calmly refocus when the mind wonders. Practicing such steps (or any number of other meditation techniques) for even a few minutes automatically brings the physiological benefits of deep stress reduction.

If you do decide to use meditation as part of your spiritual practice, it can provide an uplifting sense of connection to the Divine. Do not measure your success by your ability to hear "the voice of God," or see "visions of the Invisible." For those of us who are not spiritual geniuses, the insights and awareness that result from meditation are more subtle, but nonetheless transforming.

Many of the things I have suggested in this and other essays may be outside your comfort zone. I am only passing along what I have found valuable for me. I offer them as options to consider. Let your own experience be the judge.

"I do myself a greater injury in lying than I do to him of whom I tell a lie."

MICHEL DE MONTAIGNE (1533-1592)

Speak Your Truth

You shall not bear false witness against your neighbor. This is one of the Ten Commandments that God gave to Moses (Exodus 20:16). It is usually interpreted to have the general meaning, "do not lie." It is easy to see how this and other commandments such as "do not kill," "do not cheat on your spouse," and "do not steal" would add to social stability. Is there anything more going on here than the prophets' attempt to keep people in line—with the threat of God's punishment as motivation? If we are not afraid of God's justice, are lying and cheating smart strategies?

Allow me a slight thought detour.

Reciprocity is at the heart of primate social structure, perhaps reaching its zenith in human society. Without natural size, armor or weapons, *Homo sapiens* depended on cooperation for success. As I have discussed, helping others and sharing with others—altruism—only works as an evolutionary strategy when others return the favor and aid your own survival and reproduction. Thus, we developed an enhanced frontal cortex that can keep track of, among other things, favors owed and slights given. In other words, we keep track of "cheaters," those who are taking more than they are giving. Much of this operates at a subconscious level and may form part of the basis of why we like some people and do not like others.

This is where truthfulness comes in. When we observe someone to be honest, it builds our sense of trust in that person. When we catch people in a lie, even if it does not hurt us directly, it diminishes our trust in them. We see that person as someone who might lie to us in the future, someone who cannot be trusted for reciprocity. Our estimation of their character diminishes.

"Honesty is the best policy," not because you might go to hell, but because those around you are keeping track. The Hindu's have a concept called *Karma*. In its popular version, it means that what you put out into the world comes back to you—both good and bad. I have always thought that beyond any supernatural religious doctrine, this just made social common sense. If you treat others well, it increases the chances that they will treat you well in return. We could expand this to say that if we are a person who acts in good faith toward others—does not lie, cheat or steal—then we are seen as worthy of their altruism. We will receive more from others because they have the expectation that we will return the favor.

Cheaters are more likely to lose out in the end because they are detected and cut off from reciprocity. This is not just about lying. Talking behind other's backs, spreading rumors, taking advantage of people, showing lack of integrity—all the behaviors that express lack of character—lead to negative social consequences. The old saying: "cheaters never prosper" goes beyond moral prescription; it has a logical basis in our natural social tendencies.

Speaking the truth is a challenge because we want others to think well of us. Honesty exposes differences between people that may affect relationship. Yet, even though it may be difficult, acting with truthfulness and integrity assuredly does pay off.

In the long run, lying and cheating are not smart strategies.

Speaking your truth also includes speaking truth to yourself. This is facilitated by our habits of word choice. For example, the word "can't" is most often a substitute for "I choose not to." It is a simple avoidance of responsibility. Unless someone has physically tied you up, the statement "I can't exercise today" really means, "I choose not to exercise today."

You might argue, "I didn't choose to avoid exercise, I just didn't have time today." However, if you are completely honest, you made choices about your schedule, what time you awoke, your priorities, etc. That is why you did not exercise. If someone had said, "If you do not exercise today, you will die." chances are very good that you would have found a way to rearrange your schedule to include exercise.

We can get into the habit of thinking and speaking in ways that enable us to blame "circumstances", rather than taking responsibility for our choices that create the circumstances. We always have choice in our lives. We may not like some of the consequences of those choices (like the lowered income that comes from a job that allows more time for exercise), but it is beneficial to remind ourselves in our language and our thoughts that we are choosing the life that we are living.

Notice the difference between "I couldn't get here on time" and "I chose not to get here on time." Taking responsibility for our lives may be uncomfortable, but it is also empowering. Speaking your truth is a first step.

Language is the software of the mind. The hardware of our brain was built through a combination of genetic and environmental influences that we did not control. However, we do have some control over the software of our thoughts. The way we choose to think—the way we speak our truth to ourselves—has important consequences. Habits of thought influence our attitudes and feelings, which in turn influence our physical health. In others words, we can choose to think thoughts that make us healthier and happier.

I am not talking here about creating a fairyland of sunshine and rainbows disconnected from reality. Positive thinking is not the same thing as denial. What I am saying is that we can change our life by changing our thinking.

For example, grieving a loss is a normal human experience; something a healthy person works through, eventually emerging with acceptance. The pains of life are real and universal. When that pain becomes interminable suffering, however, we are running the wrong software.

One thing we can do to improve the language software that we run in our head is to stay in the present. Many pop psychologists have made careers out of emphasizing this concept. The past cannot be changed. The more we dwell on the negative events in our life, the more we drag ourselves down emotionally. In some cases of abuse and trauma, a qualified therapist—"software engineer"—may be necessary to work through issues that interfere with our current happiness. In most cases, obsession with negative feelings such as regret, guilt, sorrow or anger can be avoided by a healthy focus on the present.

One practice that helps keep us in the now is forgiveness. Forgiving one who has wronged us breaks a tie to the past. It does not mean condoning someone's bad behavior or labeling harmful events as acceptable. Rather, it is letting go of emotions that no longer serve us. Forgiveness is not something we do for others. Forgiveness of others is something we do for *ourselves.*

At the other end of the now continuum is the future. Obsessing about tomorrow brings worry and anxiety into today. Staying focused in the present does not mean abandonment of planning or the pleasure of anticipation. It means an acceptance of uncertainty and realization that after reasonable preparation, added worry cannot change the future.

Probably because of the skill of our mirror neurons, the stressful situations that we imagine in our future cause the release of real stress hormones in the present—and we know how chronically elevated glucocorticoid levels effect the mind and body. Focusing on the present—mindfulness—helps us avoid both suffering over the past and anxiety about the future.

A student asked, "Is there one word which may serve as a rule of practice for all of one's life?" The Master said, "Is not Reciprocity such a word?"

CONFUCIUS

Do Unto Others

Shakespeare was a writing genius. Bach was a musical genius. Michelangelo was an artistic genius. Einstein was a physics genius. Is it possible that there have been spiritual geniuses? Are some who have walked among us gifted in their ability to comprehend more of the Mystery? To me, the answer seems clearly to be yes.

I think we have to acknowledge that there is variation between people in the ability to grasp the Ungraspable. Perhaps Buddha and Jesus provide the best examples from the Eastern and Western traditions. Karl Jaspers has called them *paradigmatic personalities*. (A paradigm is an outstandingly clear example or archetype.) In the Hindu tradition, they are called *Avatars*. These individuals have taught by example as well as words. Our search for understanding can be facilitated by turning to those who embody and exemplify what human beings can be. Wisdom is manifested in the Luminaries who are awakened to their connection with the Mystery.

I do not think that any one religion or philosophy has a monopoly on The Truth. In fact, I would be suspicious of any group or organization that makes such a claim. Those who hunger for answers can always find unscrupulous individuals who are willing to provide them—at a cost. Be careful. Look for clarity of motive and purity of heart in those that you would choose to guide you on the Path. As a wise minister once told me, a trustworthy church or spiritual guide will not ask you to leave your brain in the parking lot.

I encourage you to choose a Spiritual Path that resonates with you and then work to incorporate its principles into your daily life. If God does not fit into your beliefs, adherence to humanistic ethical standards may serve the same function. The key is not which path you choose, but rather, living in integrity with the values that you adopt. There is a fundamental core at the heart of all spiritual traditions, although it is easy to be misled by doctrines that have been superimposed on the original Truth.

There are nineteen major world religions and over ten thousand subdivisions and smaller sects. Almost all help motivate their followers to lead better lives. It is time we grow in our acceptance and wisdom to realize that a faith may work for someone else even though it may not be valid for us. Any other stance stems from misguided arrogance and spiritual ignorance.

The Dalai Lama, spiritual leader of the Tibetan Buddhists, has written extensively about such tolerance and acceptance. In his book titled *How to See Yourself as You Really Are*, he explains:

"All the different religions of the world are needed to enrich human experience and world civilization. Our human minds, with all their variety, need different approaches to peace and happiness. The point is clear, humanity needs all the world's religions to suit varied ways of life, diverse spiritual needs, and inherited national traditions. All spiritual practices have love as an ideal, seek to benefit humanity and strive to make their fellows better people."

Although each religion or philosophy was written in the context of its own cultural traditions and social environment, we can learn a lot by looking for commonalities in the great spiritual teachings. One universal theme that stands out through all the Axial religions is the *Golden Rule* or *Ethic of Reciprocity*.

In Christianity, it is summarized in the words of Jesus, "*In everything do to others as you would have them do to you.*" (Matthew 7:12) In India, it is expressed as *ahimsa*, nonviolence. In China, Buddhism speaks of universal compassion, Taoism speaks of noninterference, and Confucianism speaks of brotherly love. In Greece, Platonism expresses universal ideals of virtuous behavior.

This central theme that runs through so many religions and philosophies is based on a deep understanding of the nature of humanity—our unique capacity for compassion and altruism. As social animals, it is the counterbalance to our survival instincts of competition, aggression and violence. The spiritual geniuses of the past have all been able to see that humans must consciously develop their compassionate thoughts and altruistic behaviors for the ultimate success of humankind.

There is a traditional story of a pagan who approached the revered Rabbi Hillel the Elder and said that he would convert to Judaism if the Master could recite the whole of the Torah to him while standing on one leg. Hillel replied: *"Do not do unto others as you would not have done unto you. That is the whole of the Torah: now go and learn it."*

Your Grandmother Melody was always giving to others and I saw numerous examples of the Ethic of Reciprocity at work in her life. After she became ill, we joined a brain tumor support group at our local hospital. Initially, we went to learn about treatment options, side effects of medications, clinical trials, etc. As we became more knowledgeable, we continued to go for the emotional support of individuals and couples who were sharing the same experiences.

Following weeks of radiation therapy, Melody entered an extended period of remission. We continued to attend the support group meetings, but our motivation for going changed. We saw how much it meant to the newly diagnosed members to see

Melody looking healthy and to hear her story of hope. We went to the meetings to help others—as we had been helped.

One evening during this time, we had a guest speaker who was a massage therapist and healer. Her name was Ann. Following her presentation on the benefits of massage in dealing with the physical and emotional affects of cancer treatment, she heard Melody share her story. We talked with Ann after the meeting and explained that we were grateful to be able to help others who were struggling with brain cancer. She saw Melody's caring heart and they made an instant connection.

Many months later, Melody's tumor reappeared in a more aggressive form. She began a regimen of chemotherapy that had many debilitating side effects. We sought help from Ann. To our surprise, she asked if she could work with Melody on a weekly basis—at no charge. It was a tremendous blessing for Melody during a very difficult time. Your Grandmother's compassion for others was returned to her. That is the power of reciprocity.

Here is the Ethic of Reciprocity as expressed in different faiths and philosophies from around the world:

Baha'i Faith: *"And if thine eyes be turned towards justice, choose thou for thy neighbor that which thou choosest for thyself."*
Epistle to the Son of the Wolf

Buddhism: *"Hurt not others in ways that you yourself would find hurtful."*   Udana-Varga 5:18

Christianity: *"In everything do to others as you would have them do to you;"*   Matthew 7:12 ("unto" in old King James)

Confucianism: *"Do not do to others what you do not want them to do to you."*   Analects 15:23

Ancient Egyptian: *"Do for one who may do for you, that you may cause him thus to do."*   Tale of the Eloquent Peasant
(Perhaps the earliest version of the Ethic of Reciprocity—1800 BCE.)

Hinduism: *"This is the sum of duty: do not do to others what would cause pain if done to you."*   Mahabharata 5:1517

Islam: *"None of you truly believes until he wishes for his brother what he wishes for himself."*   Number 13 of Imam

Janism: *"A man should wander about treating all creatures as he himself would be treated."*   Sutrakritanga 1.11.33

Judaism: *"What is hateful to you, do not do to your fellow man."*   Talmud, Shabbat 31a

Native American: *"Do not wrong or hate your neighbor, for in doing so, you wrong yourself."*   Pima Proverb

Roman Paganism: *"The law imprinted on the hearts of all men is to love the members of society as themselves."*

Shinto: *"The heart of the person before you is a mirror. See there your own form."*   Munetada Kurozumi

Sikhism: *"Don't create enmity with anyone as God is within everyone."*   Guru Arjan Devji 259

Taoism: *"Regard your neighbor's gain as your own gain, your neighbor's loss as your own loss."*   T'ai Shang Kan Ying P'ien

Zoroastrianism: *"Whatever is disagreeable to yourself do not do unto others."*   Shayast-na-Shayast 13:29

Greek Philosophy:
"Do not do to others that which would anger you if others did it to you."   Socrates 5th century BCE

Humanism: *"Don't do things you wouldn't want to have done to you."*   British Humanist Society

There is no more important wisdom.

The Dalai Lama has written:

From my own limited experience, I have found that the greatest degree of inner tranquility comes from the development of love and compassion. The more we care for the happiness of others, the greater our own sense of well-being becomes...

Ultimately, the reason why love and compassion bring us the greatest happiness is simply that our nature cherishes them above all else. The need for love lies at the very foundation of human existence. It results from the profound interdependence we share with one another.

In My Own Words 2008

This seems like an appropriate place to share my favorite Christian prayer. It is often called the Prayer of Saint Francis of Assisi, although the history of the prayer cannot be traced all the way back to his lifetime (1181-1226 CE).

> *Lord, make me an instrument of your peace.*
> *Where there is hatred, let me sow love.*
> *Where there is injury, pardon.*
> *Where there is doubt, faith.*
> *Where there is despair, hope.*
> *Where there is darkness, light.*
> *Where there is sadness, joy.*
>
> *O Divine Master,*
> *grant that I may not so much seek to be consoled,*
> *as to console;*
> *to be understood, as to understand;*
> *to be loved, as to love.*
> *For it is in giving that we receive.*
> *It is in pardoning that we are pardoned,*
> *and it is in dying that we are born to Eternal Life.*
>
> *Amen.*

"We must adjust to changing times and still hold to unchanging principles."

PRESIDENT JIMMY CARTER

Live In Principle

In an age where traditional religions are losing their grip on large parts of society, we must ask a pivotal question. Does being "good" and behaving ethically make sense if we do not believe in a judgmental God who controls the elevator to heaven and hell?

In my experience, the answer is affirmative. Certain types of positive behavior are imbedded in our human nature. Just as "speaking your truth" has long-term rewards in our relationships, "living in principle" has both interpersonal and intrapersonal benefits. Others note our integrity and treat us accordingly. Holding ourselves to high standards ultimately reduces our suffering and increases our happiness and fulfillment.

In the twenty-first century, the voice of God may not speak to us from a burning bush to tell us how to behave. However, we can look to our highest human nature for clues. Undertaken with a perceptive mind and open heart, what emerges from this exploration are *Wisdom Principles* for living.

The great spiritual mystics provide guidance for us here. But whether they come from the Buddha, the Bible, the Bhagavad Gita or the Qur'an, it is essential to find the purity of the original insights regarding our best behavioral options. Seek Principles that ring true at the core of your own being.

It is one thing to adopt high personal standards; it is another to live up to them. Even saints struggle with the devil of desire and the tugs of temptation. Our multiple mind modules have their own agendas, and some of them lobby for selfishness. We cannot deny our evolutionary past in which aggression and competition were necessary for survival.

What we can do is work for incremental improvement. We may not adhere to our Principles all the time in every situation, but we can hold that as our goal and strive to express the best part of our nature. This allows us to tip the scales in favor of our compassionate and altruistic tendencies.

Love is a Wisdom Principle. Any concept of God that I can imagine includes a Loving Presence in the world. The great exemplars like Jesus have taught us to be expressions of that Loving Presence. Our ability to love is a hallmark of our humanity. In all its various forms, love is the foundation upon which the other Wisdom Principles stand.

Acceptance is a Principle that nurtures the growth of Love. This is one area where the biological concept of variation is useful to us. People are different. Nature has designed people to be different. Accepting that others cannot help but be different from us is fundamental.

We may not like (or even get along with) many other people because they have different values, beliefs and behaviors. Accepting those differences with kindhearted understanding opens the door to maintaining a loving attitude in our interactions with all people.

Compassion is an expression of loving acceptance. Even though we are different from others in many ways, at the core of every person is a humanity that we all share. Compassion flows from a recognition of this shared humanity, for we can understand the pain of others and empathize with their life struggles.

Love and acceptance are attitudes that we carry with us, while compassion is expressed at its highest level in our behaviors. Comforting those in pain; protecting those in danger; sharing with those in need—these are the actions of one who chooses to practice the Principle of Compassion.

Peace is a related Principle. Being an expression of Peace in the world goes beyond the restraint of violence. It is the active embodiment of empathy and compassion in dealing with all people. Some people exude peace in their choice of both words and actions. Such gentle souls act like social soundproofing, reducing the aggressive noise and promoting the quiet harmony of cooperation.

One aspect of Peace is harmlessness, and we can set that as our intention in our interactions with nature as well as with people. Albert Schweitzer exemplifies living in the Wisdom Principle of Peace. Born on the German-French border in 1875, he earned a doctorate in theology, was a respected music scholar and a talented organist. Early in his life, he committed to pursuing his personal interests until the age of thirty and then giving the rest of his life to serving humanity, with Jesus as his example.

In 1905, he followed through by returning to school for six years to earn his medical degree. He then traveled deep into equatorial West Africa to establish a missionary hospital. At great personal sacrifice, he and his wife served the needs of the local people over several decades. In 1952, Albert Schweitzer was awarded the Nobel Peace Prize for both his humanitarian efforts and a philosophy that he developed and wrote about called *Reverence for Life*.

Schweitzer summarized his philosophy in this quotation: *"A man is truly ethical only when he obeys the compulsion to help all life which he is able to assist, and shrinks from injuring anything that lives."* Anecdotal stories indicate that Schweitzer lived his philosophy by refusing to step on ants or swat flies. In another famous quote he said, *"Constant kindness can accomplish much. As the sun makes ice melt, kindness causes misunderstanding, mistrust and hostility to evaporate."* Such is the power of living in the Principle of Peace.

Service is another Wisdom Principle exemplified by Dr. Schweitzer. When our lives feel empty or unrewarding, the antidote is choosing to dedicate ourselves to being of service. One way of accomplishing this is by choosing a career that allows us to help others. Most jobs can be thought of as expressions of service if approached with the right attitude and perspective. Of course, there are also many ways to be of service outside of the work environment, including the high calling of serving our family.

Choice is a powerful Principle. Humanity has been given the extraordinary gifts of awareness and free will. Unlike any other living creature, we have the freedom of choice in each moment we live and that gives us a life of infinite possibilities. We do not always choose our circumstances, and the events that surround us may be unpredictable and hurtful, but we can always choose our response and way forward.

This makes us responsible for our own life and our own feelings. Happiness is a choice, or perhaps more accurately, the result of our ongoing choices. If we live in Principle, we make choices that keep us in the natural flow of life that automatically brings happiness. This may require that we stand against the prevailing social currents, testing our personal strength and interpersonal courage, but it is ultimately our wisest choice.

Sometimes our most life enhancing choices involve risk. In this context, I do not mean the life and death risks of sky diving or jumping off cliffs. I mean risk of failure. Change involves risk, whether it is finding a new job, moving to a new city or beginning a new relationship. Every new adventure carries some risk of failure—not getting what you want. Nevertheless, *the risk of failure if you do not try is one hundred percent!* Many of my most satisfying life changes have required me to overcome anxiety and fear in order to have the chance for greater happiness and fulfillment. Let me give you just two examples.

In sixth grade, I had a wonderful teacher named Mr. Bracone. He was my first male teacher, full of energy, creativity and caring. After seeing the joy on his face as he taught our class, I knew I wanted to become a teacher when I grew up.

In high school, I discovered something else about myself. I was terrified of public speaking. Having to give an oral report was a near death experience for me. I began to doubt my ability to be a successful teacher.

Fortunately, my desire to become a teacher was stronger than my fear. I decided I needed to take some risks to achieve my goal and I signed up for public speaking classes in both high school and college. Every speech I gave made the next speech *slightly* easier. The risk I took of facing my fears paid off in a very satisfying career as an educator.

Some of our biggest risks involve relationships. A year after your Grandmother Melody passed away; I decided to go to my fortieth high school reunion. There I had a nice conversation with a woman who had been a good friend decades ago, but with whom I had not spoken in over twenty years. I was surprised to learn that her spouse also had passed away a few years earlier. I was even more surprised that I found myself attracted to her.

The evening was over too quickly, and the next day I couldn't stop thinking about her. She lived an eight-hour drive away and we had only talked for a short time, but I felt unfinished. The idea of reaching out to her was scary—I feared rejection and hurt feelings. Yet something told me that the opportunity for relationship, whether it was renewed friendship or something more, was worth the risk of "failure." I sent her an email.

As you probably know, that woman is your Nanny Carolyn. She became my wife when you were just a baby.

Take some risks in your life when your intuition tells you it is right. If you are living in Principle and are applying your passion, you will succeed more often than you might imagine.

Laughter may seem like an odd Wisdom Principle. As we strive to uplift ourselves by living in Principle, we must always maintain our sense of humor. We have to laugh at our own foibles because our evolutionary history and accidental culture lead us to behave in such odd ways. We must also laugh at our circumstances, trying as we do to make sense of an existence that is beyond our understanding.

In addition to his wisdom and compassion, His Holiness The Dalai Lama is known for his child-like laugh. *Laughter is an expression of deep understanding.* Laughter, the kind that bubbles over from effervescent happiness, is also an expression of the highest level of joy. This kind of laughter (as opposed to the shock laughter elicited by some comedians) is an expression of child-like playfulness and something to cherish. The release of heart-felt laughter has both psychological and physiological benefits. Seek a good laugh as often as you can.

Like a child, a wise person plays a lot and laughs a lot, enjoying the full measure of the precious gift of life.

Gratitude is the final Wisdom Principle I want to mention. Choosing to live in a state of gratitude shows an awareness of the truth about existence. Life is a blessing.

A child expresses gratitude with every smile as she or he enjoys the simple things in life—a hug, a game of peek-a-boo, or seeing a bird in a tree. We can learn from their wide-eyed sense of appreciation. Beginning each morning with a grateful heart and carrying that attitude with us throughout the day returns profound benefits. *To be truly wise is to live in deep gratitude.*

Living in Principle takes effort. If you begin by living a principled life from belief, your experiences may allow it to grow in strength to become faith. Only then will you know it is worth the effort. I encourage you to try living in alignment with these Wisdom Principles—and see what happens!

"I know God will not give me anything I can't handle. I just wish that He didn't trust me so much."

Practice Your Wisdom

Thomas Jefferson created his own Bible by cutting the words of Jesus from the four gospels of the New Testament and pasting them together in chronological order. His goal was to find the purity of the wisdom teachings of Jesus without the supernatural aspects and misinterpretations added by the gospel writers. In 1813, he described his efforts in a letter to John Adams. *"In extracting the pure principles which he taught, we should have to strip off the artificial vestments in which they have been muffled by priests, who have travestied them into various forms, as instruments of riches and power to themselves...There will be found remaining the most sublime and benevolent code of morals which has ever been offered to man."*

In this essay, I have selected some of my favorite quotes from Matthew. It is not my intention to imply that the wisdom contained in Christianity is superior to that found in other spiritual traditions. Yet, whether you believe these words were spoken by the Son of God, a Divinely inspired prophet, or just a gifted teacher, the lessons represent timeless wisdom.

5: 14 "You are the light of the world. A city built on a hill cannot be hid. ¹⁵No one after lighting a lamp puts it under the bushel basket, but on the lampstand, and it gives light to all in the house. ¹⁶In the same way, let your light shine before others, so that they may see your good works and give glory to your Father in heaven."

The foregoing words encourage me to stand by my values even when it is socially uncomfortable. Openly living in Principle supports others to express their highest nature and attracts like-minded people who may in turn support you.

5:21 "You have heard that it was said to those of ancient times, 'You shall not murder'; and 'whoever murders shall be liable to judgment.' ²²But I say to you that if you are angry with a brother or sister, you will be liable to judgment; and if you insult a brother or sister, you will be liable to the council; and if you say, 'You fool,' you will be liable to the hell of fire.

²³So when you are offering your gift at the altar, if you remember that your brother or sister has something against you, ²⁴leave your gift there before the altar and go; first be reconciled to your brother or sister, and then come and offer your gift."

Forgiveness breaks the cycle of retribution. It is a prerequisite for living with a peaceful heart. I interpret these words to mean that prayer and piety are hypocritical if I do not practice my beliefs in my daily life with the people around me. (I am sure my younger brother wishes I had learned this earlier in life—before I teased and tortured him mercilessly when we were children.)

5:38 "You have heard that it was said, 'An eye for an eye and a tooth for a tooth.' ³⁹But I say to you, Do not resist an evildoer. But if anyone strikes you on the right cheek, turn the other also; ⁴⁰and if anyone wants to sue you and take your coat, give your cloak as well; ⁴¹and if anyone forces you to go one mile, go also the second mile. ⁴²Give to everyone who begs from you, and do not refuse anyone who wants to borrow from you."

5:43 "You have heard that it was said, 'You shall love your neighbor and hate your enemy.' ⁴⁴But I say to you, Love your enemies and pray for those who persecute you, ⁴⁵so that you may be children of your Father in heaven; for he makes his sun rise on the evil and on the good, and sends rain on the righteous and on the unrighteous. ⁴⁶For if you love those who love you, what reward do you have? Do not even the tax collectors do the same? ⁴⁷And if you greet only your brothers and sisters, what more are you doing than others? Do not even the Gentiles do the same?"

Jesus sets the bar very high in the previous two passages. He is challenging us to overcome our natural tendencies for retaliation. Staying centered in the Principles of Love and Peace requires tremendous strength and moment-by-moment mindfulness.

6:19 "Do not store up for yourselves treasures on earth, where moth and rust consume and where thieves break in and steal; ²⁰but store up for yourselves treasures in heaven, where neither moth nor rust consumes and where thieves do not break in and steal. ²¹For where your treasure is, there your heart will be also."

6: 24 "No one can serve two masters; for a slave will either hate the one and love the other, or be devoted to the one and despise the other. You cannot serve God and wealth."

19:24 "Again I tell you, it is easier for a camel to go through the eye of a needle than for someone who is rich to enter the kingdom of God."

In a society that increasingly seeks happiness in material wealth, these words ring more true than ever. I never thought that Jesus was against money, only that he was warning us about the consequences of misplaced priorities. For me, "heaven" and "kingdom of God" refer to a contented state of mind resulting from living in Principle.

Poverty does not bring happiness, but neither does focusing all of our time and energy on gaining more wealth.

6:25 "Therefore I tell you, do not worry about your life, what you will eat or what you will drink, or about your body, what you will wear. Is not life more than food, and the body more than clothing? ²⁶Look at the birds of the air; they neither sow nor reap nor gather into barns, and yet your heavenly Father feeds them. Are you not of more value than they?

27And can any of you by worrying add a single hour to your span of life? 28And why do you worry about clothing? Consider the lilies of the field, how they grow; they neither toil nor spin, 29yet I tell you, even Solomon in all his glory was not clothed like one of these. 30But if God so clothes the grass of the field, which is alive today and tomorrow is thrown into the oven, will he not much more clothe you--you of little faith? 31Therefore do not worry, saying, 'What will we eat?' or 'What will we drink?' or 'What will we wear?'"

6: 34 "So do not worry about tomorrow, for tomorrow will bring worries of its own. Today's trouble is enough for today."

No pop psychology book ever made a better case for living in the present and living with a sense of trust. In my experience, striving to live in Principle brings good things into my life. Worry has never brought me anything but harmful stress hormones.

A common misinterpretation of the previous quotation (Matthew 6:25-34) is that if we are good enough to *deserve* it, we can sit back and God will provide for all of our needs. This represents a very simple-minded view of God's interaction with human beings and sets us up for disillusionment.

By giving us the gift of free will, God also gives us responsibility for our own life. To paraphrase Paul's letter to the Galatians (6:7-8), we reap what we sow. Consider the following:

7:7 "Ask, and it will be given you; search, and you will find; knock, and the door will be opened for you. 8For everyone who asks receives, and everyone who searches finds, and for everyone who knocks, the door will be opened. 9Is there anyone among you who, if your child asks for bread, will give a stone? 10Or if the child asks for a fish, will give a snake?"

Notice that the quotation includes active words like "ask", "search", and "knock". *"Pray, then find a way"* might be an appropriate summary motto. Or, in a more traditional phrase (that is not in the Bible), *"God helps those who help themselves."*

7 "Do not judge, so that you may not be judged. ²For with the judgment you make you will be judged, and the measure you give will be the measure you get. ³Why do you see the speck in your neighbor's eye, but do not notice the log in your own eye? ⁴Or how can you say to your neighbor, 'Let me take the speck out of your eye,' while the log is in your own eye? ⁵You hypocrite, first take the log out of your own eye, and then you will see clearly to take the speck out of your neighbor's eye."

This has always been one of my favorite Bible quotes. When I find myself judging others, it often pops into my mind. We are all imperfect. Judging others says more about us—our beliefs, values and desires—than it says about the other person. We are better served focusing our energy on our own needs for improvement. Unless asked, the best advice we can offer others is through our example.

7:12 "In everything do to others as you would have them do to you; for this is the law and the prophets."
22:36 "Teacher, which commandment in the law is the greatest?" ³⁷He said to him, 'You shall love the Lord your God with all your heart, and with all your soul, and with all your mind.' ³⁸This is the greatest and first commandment. ³⁹And a second is like it: 'You shall love your neighbor as yourself.'

As I noted in a previous essay, following the Golden Rule (Ethic of Reciprocity) is not just about being good to earn your way to heaven. When we observe that someone in our social group behaves altruistically, we know that our interactions with them are safe—and we learn to trust them. Earning this trust from our peers leads to interpersonal rewards in the here and now.

Treating others as we would like to be treated is not a sacrifice. On the contrary, treating others well operates in our own best interest. It is also the most fundamental Principle for the betterment of society.

7:13 "Enter through the narrow gate; for the gate is wide and the road is easy that leads to destruction, and there are many who take it. ¹⁴For the gate is narrow and the road is hard that leads to life, and there are few who find it."

Robert Frost echoed a similar theme in his famous poem *The Road Not Taken:*

> Two roads diverged in a wood, and I–
> I took the one less traveled by,
> And that has made all the difference.

Living with wisdom is not the common path. It is not the easy path. I am only recommending it because, for me, it has made all the difference.

Epilogue

Dear Adam,

That's it. That's all the wisdom I've got.
(Probably more than you wanted to read!)

I strongly believe that the solutions to all of our problems, from personal to global, are available to us through education and choice. I have shared these essays in the hope that you will choose a path that makes you part of the solution—and encourages others to do the same by your example.

Real wisdom is timeless, based on a human nature that evolved over the millennia. It emphasizes our connections to the natural world and to each other. It moves us to think and behave with compassion and altruism—the best sides of our human nature.

I have been thinking of you with love as I wrote these pages. I hope you have found some value in them.

Life is an indescribable blessing. Enjoy.

With Love,
Grampy

Bibliography

One thing I have discovered in the process of writing this book is an abundance of humility. Gifted writers have shared volumes of valuable wisdom in the following works, which I have sampled as resources for these essays. If you want to go deeper into the topics introduced here, I recommend these books to begin your exploration.

Armstrong, K *A History of God* Ballantine Books (1993)

Armstrong, K *The Great Transformation* Anchor Books (2006)

Barrett, L *Human Evolutionary Psychology* Princeton University Press (2002)

Benson, H *The Relaxation Response* William Morrow Co(1975)

Bryson, B *A Short History of Nearly Everything* Broadway Books (2003)

Campbell, N *Biology* Benjamin/Cummings (1999)

Collins, F *The Language of God* Free Press (2006)

Darwin, C *The Origin of Species* Random House (1979)

Dawkins, R *The Ancestor's Tale* Mariner Books (2004)

Dawkins, R *The God Delusion* Mariner Books (2006)

Dawkins, R *The Greatest Show on Earth* Free Press (2009)

Dawkins, R *The Selfish Gene* Oxford University Press (2006)

Diamond, J *The Third Chimpanzee* HarperCollins (1992)

Dunbar, R *Evolutionary Psychology* Oneworld Pub (2007)

Emerson, R *Emerson's Essays* Harper & Row (1926)

Feiler, B *Abraham* HarperCollins Publishers (2002)

Feiler, B *Where God Was Born* HarperCollins Publishers (2005)

Fromm, E *The Art of Loving* Harper & Row (1956)

Gilbert, M *The Disposable Male* The Hunter Press (2006)

Hanson, Rick *Buddha's Brain* New Harbinger Publications (2009)

Holmes, E *The Science of Mind* Putnam's Sons (1938)

Bibliography

Huber, R *The Bible Through The Ages* Reader's Digest (1996)

Iacoboni, M *Mirroring People* Picador (2008)

Johnson, T *Finding God in the Questions* InterVarsity Press (2004)

Keirsey, D/Bates, M *Please Understand Me* Promethean Books (1978)

Keirsey, D *Please Understand Me II* Prometheus Nemesis Book Co (1998)

King, B *Biological Anthropology: An Evolutionary Perspective* College of William and Mary (Lecture 2002)

Lipton, B *The Biology of Belief* Elite Books (2005)

Maslow, A *Toward a Psychology of Being* Nostrand Co (1962)

Metzger, B/Murphy, R (Editors) *The New Oxford Annotated Bible* (New Revised Standard Version) Oxford University Press (1991)

Montagu, A *Growing Young* McGraw Hill (1981)

Ornstein, R *Multimind* Houghton Mifflin Co (1986)

Ornstein, R/Ehrlich, P *New World New Mind* Doubleday (1989)

Roizen, M/Oz, M *You, the Owner's Manual* HarperCollins (2005)

Sapolsky, R *Biology and Human Behavior* Stanford University (Lecture 2005)

Sapolsky, R *Why Zebras Don't Get Ulcers* W.H. Freeman (1998)

Silver, L *The Science of Self* Princeton University (Lecture 2009)

Smith, L *Illustrated Timeline of Religion* Sterling Publishing (2007)

Tippett, K *Einstein's God* Penguin Books (2010)

The Dalai Lama *In My Own Words* Hay House (2008)

Thoreau, H *Thoreau: Walden and Other Writings* Bantam (1962)

Willett, W *Eat, Drink, and Be Healthy* Fireside (2001)

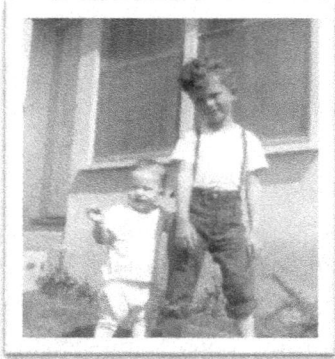

This is a photo of your Grampy before he developed enough wisdom to know that suspenders and rolled up pants are not a good fashion statement.

Younger brother John prefers his own style.

In this mid-life photo, your Grampy is captured in the frantic search for wisdom. No one ever said wisdom came easily.

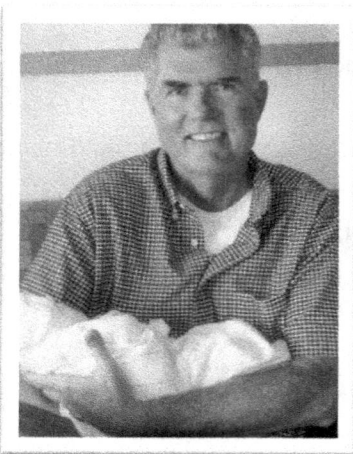

Here, your Grampy holds you for the first time, shortly after your birth.

Every time he would start to share his wisdom, you would fall asleep.

Grampy decided he had better write a book.

Also by R. Wayne Morgan

Happy Birthday – You're Old:
A Boomer's Guide to Aging and Other Unexpected Developments

Sure, I Can Do That:
A Twentieth Century American Memoir

The Fermata Chronicle:
A Novella of the Next Age

The first is available in paperback. All three are available as eBooks (as is this book). Just search on your favorite bookseller's website for R. Wayne Morgan.

Feel free to send comments, or questions to:
rwaynemorgan@comcast.net

www.ingramcontent.com/pod-product-compliance
Lightning Source LLC
Chambersburg PA
CBHW070952040426
42443CB00007B/474